Graeme Lay

# Inside the Cannibal Pot

NEW
HOLLAND

## ALSO BY GRAEME LAY

### NOVELS AND SHORT STORY COLLECTIONS
*The Mentor*
*The Fools on the Hill*
*Temptation Island*
*Dear Mr Cairney*
*Motu Tapu: Stories of the South Pacific*
*The Town on the Edge of the World*
*Alice & Luigi*

### YOUNG ADULT NOVELS
*The Wave Rider*
*Leaving One Foot Island*
*Return to One Foot Island*
*The Pearl of One Foot Island*

### CHILDREN
*Are We There Yet? A Kiwi Kid's Holiday Exploring Guide*
*Nanny Potaka's Birthday Treat*

### TRAVEL
*Passages: Journeys in Polynesia*
*Pacific New Zealand*
*The Cook Islands* (with Ewan Smith)
*New Zealand: A Visual Celebration* (with Gareth Eyres)
*Samoa* (with Evotia Tamua)
*Feasts and Festivals* (with Glenn Jowitt)
*The Magic of New Zealand* (with Holger Leue)
*The Globetrotter Guide to New Zealand*
*The Best of Auckland*
*Auckland and Beyond* (with Holger Leue)
*New Zealand: the Magnificent Journey* (with Gareth Eyres)
*The Miss Tutti Frutti Contest: Travel Tales of the South Pacific*
*The Globetrotter Travel Atlas of New Zealand*

### EDITOR
*Metro Fiction*
*100 New Zealand Short Short Stories*
*Another 100 New Zealand Short Short Stories*
*The Third Century*
*Boys' Own Stories*
*50 Short Short Stories by Young New Zealanders*
*An Affair of the Heart: A Celebration of Frank Sargeson's Centenary* (with Stephen Stratford)
*Golden Weather: North Shore Writers Past & Present* (with Jack Ross)
*Home: New Short Short Stories by New Zealand Writers* (with Stephen Stratford)
*The New Zealand Book of the Beach*

# CONTENTS

# Introduction

The queue wound its way around the cordoned-off, passengers-only zone, very, very slowly. Those at the front of the queue peeled off, then traipsed up to whichever check-in counter represented their destination in French Polynesia: Bora Bora, Huahine, Rangiroa or the Marquesas. I hauled my suitcase along beside me, at the same time trying to keep the pack on my back balanced. I had been unable to find a luggage trolley at Papeete Airport, and both bags were very heavy, containing large numbers of my unsold books, which I seldom travel without. Pinioned tightly under my left arm were my tickets and passport. It was only eight o'clock in the morning, but already it was very hot. Many of the Tahitian women in the queue were waving pandanus fans back and forth in front of their faces. Fanless myself, I was discomforted by the trickles of sweat running down inside my shirt.

The queue continued to move forward slowly, like glue oozing from a tube. But at least, I rationalised, it is oozing. The four check-in counters were now within reach. Then the family of four in front of me was beckoned forward. Grabbing the handle of my suitcase, I moved up to fill the vacuum they had left. As I did so the case overbalanced and fell over, striking my ankle. As I bent over to bring the case upright, my back-pack slewed and its strap wrenched my neck. Staggering upright, I adjusted the suitcase and the back-pack. I was sweating heavily now, but I had reached the head of the queue. At last I was the next to be called; at last I could be shot of these bloody bags. Between me and the check-in counters up ahead was a large clear area, demarcated by a red line painted on the floor. In just minutes I would be arriving at my first destination, the check-in counter.

Then, out of the corner of my right eye, I saw a trolley appear from somewhere. Piled high with brocade-patterned suitcases, it was being pushed by a pretty young Tahitian woman in a tightly fitting pareu. Beside the trolley strode a middle-aged European man, stylishly dressed in dark blue chinos, a green long-sleeved shirt and tan boat shoes. For an instant I thought he looked familiar, but a second later he had his back to me, *and was standing calmly alongside his trolley at the check-in counter ahead of me.* For a moment I stood completely still in disbelief. The bastard had jumped not just me, but the *entire queue.* Who the hell did he think he was? In my mind queue jumpers are right up there with suicide bombers, literary theoreticians and people who shove their aircraft seats right back into your face.

Hauling my case after me, trying not to drop my travel documents, I went directly up to the man, set my case down and tapped him on his left shoulder, hard. When he turned, I drew myself up to my full height, leaned forward and said slowly, 'You-are-not-entitled-to-be-there.   I-was-the-next-in-line-in-the-queue-and-*you-have-jumped-it.* What-on-earth-gives-*you*-the right to do that?' The man at least had the decency to flinch with embarrassment. He was of medium height, his longish dark hair had been neatly brushed into place and his clothes as already noted were very stylish. A bemused expression crossed his freshly shaven face, then he said, sounding more surprised than apologetic, 'Well, it wasn't really me. I was just following my assistant. She led the way.' He waved a hand at the girl in the pareu, who was handing his travel documents over to the woman at the check-in counter.

Now it was my turn to be confused. The man's voice was well modulated, and carried the trace of an Irish accent. I *had* seen him before, many times, although we had never previously met. It was the actor, Pierce Brosnan, and he was even better looking in the flesh than he was on the screen. His eyes twinkled as he observed in my expression the surprise which he must have seen countless times around the world. 'I'm very sorry, but as I said, I just follow my guide.' Again he waved his hand towards the girl. At all four check-in counters, the Air Tahiti staff were whispering and giggling. *It's him, it's Pierce Brosnan. But who's the grumpy old guy he's arguing with?*

'Look,' Pierce went on, waving his hand airily, 'there's a free counter. You can go there.'

Glancing to the right and now feeling more than a little foolish, I saw that the woman at the Rangiroa check-in counter was beckoning me forward. I nodded briskly. 'Right, I will.' And pulling my wobbling case after me, still aware of Pierce's bemused expression, I staggered off towards the counter. The woman there was aged about 40, plumpish, with a frangipani flower behind one ear. As she took my tickets and passport I asked her, thinking that to have the famous actor's company on the atoll could be interesting, 'Is Mr Brosnan going to Rangiroa too?'

The woman shook her head. 'No he's going to Bora Bora. He's got a place there.' She giggled like a girl. 'He gave me his autograph last time he came through.'

My case and back-pack were placed on the scales, labelled, and I was handed my boarding pass. Still disconcerted, I glanced to my left at the neighbouring check-in counter, where Pierce was being handed his documents and boarding pass. Catching my eye, he gave me a grin, a wave, then turned away, trying to ignore the scores of transfixed expressions from the people still waiting in the queue behind him.

That incident seems to me to typify today's world of travel: tedious, uncomfortable, overcrowded, but always with the capacity to surprise, and occasionally, to delight. An hour later, as I was staring out the window of the banking plane at the sublimely beautiful mountains, reef and bays of the island of Moorea, bound for the equally stunning atoll of Rangiroa, all the previous tedium was forgiven.

After all, how many people get to take James Bond on and survive to tell the tale?

# Travelling by Numbers

When you last travelled, was the airport car-park crowded? Did you find that the queues at the check-in counter went on forever? Was the departure lounge congested? Was every seat on the plane taken? All this was true last time I went anywhere. Sometimes it seems that half the world's population is on the move.

It almost is. Every year, nearly a billion people visit a foreign country. Travel has for years been the world's largest industry, and global tourism is growing at a rate of between four and five percent a year. The desire to travel is, evidently, insatiable.

Why? Why do hundreds of millions of people pay thousands of millions of dollars to exchange the comfort and security of home for the uncertainties, risks and expense of foreign places? They do so because of a potent combination of push and pull factors. Day-to-day lives are humdrum. At home family is infuriating, work is boring, work-mates are insufferable, the boss detestable and it rains too much. The only thing that makes day-to-day life tolerable is the thought of travel to come. After all, overseas the sun is shinier, the sea bluer, the night-life wilder.

Overseas women are more beautiful, the food is tastier, the music more vibrant, traditions wiser, customs quainter, morals laxer.

This is the way 'overseas' is marketed, and it works. Glossy advertisements depict overseas as a place where dull day-to-day experiences are exchanged for the exhilaration of the exotic. Travel is romantic, the journey thrilling, the destinations enchanting. Overseas is not only different, it is incomparably superior to home. Most travel advertising floats these fantasies before us. Thus, much of travel is dreaming. A man I knew who was given only months to live decided that before he died he had to fulfil a long-held fantasy. 'I'm going to go to Las Vegas,' he told me. 'I'm going to play the roulette tables there and sniff cocaine from a hooker's navel. If I can make it.' He did, and although he died far too young, when he did so shortly afterwards he was less unhappy than he would have been had he not travelled and fulfilled his fantasies.

That most of the temptations dangled before the traveller's eyes prove illusory is not the slightest deterrent to international travel. Some of the unhappiest people I have ever seen have been on their trip-of-a-lifetime. Yet human nature being what it is, the disagreeable experiences fade quickly in the memory and the pleasant ones become better with every showing of the holiday photographs. (There's a name for this phenomenon. Academics who study the vacation mentality – yes, there is such a subject – call it 'rosy retrospection'.) And before the traveller leaves home there is usually an 'over the rainbow' quality to the departure, a strong element of hopeful escapism. The allure of the exotic, however phony, remains irresistible. Indeed, most of the pleasure of travel lies in its anticipation. The first thing a traveller packs is rose-tinted glasses.

So which people do the most travelling? The Japanese, perhaps? The Americans? No. Back in 2003 the Germans overtook the Americans as the most travelled nationality (86.6 million trips abroad), which may not come as a surprise to anyone who's shared a beach in Turkey, Italy or Spain with thousands of colourless, overweight burghers from Berlin or Bavaria, recalling that dark joke circulating after the Air France Concorde crash in 2000, which killed 111 German holiday-makers. The joke? So many German tourists, so few Concordes ...

(A tourist and a traveller are quite different creatures. A traveller is a person who undertakes a journey in a spirit of inquiry, who relishes the entire experience of different places and people. Tourists just visit. As another observer has put it, 'Travellers make their own way, whereas tourists' paths have been beaten into submission long before they go.' It's understandable, therefore, that the word 'tourist' now has pejorative overtones and that tourists themselves are often the objects of derision. Tourists are holiday-makers, usually content to show no curiosity about their destination beyond the immediate gratifications it offers them. To put it unkindly, as poet Kevin Ireland – no stranger to the departure lounge himself – has written: 'Tourist travel narrows the mind and broadens the prejudices. Tourism is busloads of glum tourists whizzing around the countryside, getting the fingers-up sign from the locals and being bullied and fleeced by rapacious operators. And the effect is a two-way process: I've known many people who've come back from foreign lands with their phobias fed and their fears fattened.' Harsh, but true. And for that reason this book will concentrate on travelling, rather than touristing.

The English are in second place as global travellers with 65.3 million trips abroad and the Americans third (58.3 million). The latter figure seems surprising, considering that less than 20 percent of Americans hold a passport. Those who do, however, evidently put them to frequent use. But the Germans and the English won't hold the lead in the global travel stakes for much longer.

Travel trends show that, as in other matters, the Japanese and the Chinese are rising fast. By 2020, provided that their economies don't implode in the interim, the world's most frequent travellers will be from Japan and China.

And where are they off to, these hundreds of millions of perpetually moving people? Mainly to the Old World, with its sophistication, style, traditions and ancient buildings. Of the New World, only the US makes it into the top four destinations. The world's favourite tourist destinations, in order of popularity, are France, Spain, the US and Italy. Europe received 444 million arrivals in 2005, followed a long way back by the Asia-Pacific region with 156 million arrivals and the Americas with 133 million. And although the Middle East and Africa are synonymous with war, religious hatred, famine and infectious diseases, they still draw significant numbers of visitors. During 2005 the Middle East had 38 million visitors and Africa had 36 million. In some parts of the world, the number of locals is eclipsed by foreign visitors. Islands perceived as desirable destinations are particularly prone to tourist inundations. Rarotonga, for example, which has a circumference of 32km and a permanent population of just 9000, receives over 60,000 foreign visitors every year. Sometimes on the island it's hard to spot a genuine local.

Some places have become impossibly congested with these travelling hordes; places such as the Louvre, St Marks Square, Piccadilly Circus, the Spanish Steps, Hong Kong Island's Peak tram. As soon as you get there, you want to get away. And if you want to avoid other people when flying, keep away from Atlanta's Hartsfield-Jackson Airport. It's the world's busiest, with 79 million passengers passing through it every year. The North Atlantic is the world's busiest long-haul corridor, and London-New York is the busiest long-haul air route, with 2.3 million people flying between the two cities annually. London-Dublin is the busiest short-haul route in the world, testimony to the drawing power of those two great cities.

The perilous state of the world usually has little lasting effect on travel. International travellers, it seems, are only temporarily deterred by crises of one sort or another. In 2005 it was bird flu. Now a couple of years on, it's 'what bird flu?' On Boxing Day 2004, much of coastal South-East Asia was devastated by a tsunami. A couple of Boxing Days on and the resorts of Thailand are again seething with tourists. Dreadful terrorist attacks on trains in London and Madrid leave hundreds dead and maimed, but the effect on tourist visits to those cities is fleeting. And when the price of aviation fuel soars? Budget airlines still offer cheap, albeit body-hugging, plane seats. It seems that no murderous bombing, no oil crisis, no natural disaster, no pandemic is powerful enough to deter international travel for long (although I have sometimes wondered what strategic plan the Iraqi Tourism Minister is working on). To give just one example, during 2005, 86 million people – a 7.6 percent increase on the previous year – visited Florida, in spite of that state reeling from hurricanes Gavin, Katrina, Rita and Wilma in the same year.

International travellers can afford to be fickle, given that they have so much choice. Post-Communist Russia, a few years ago a trendy destination, has lately become too expensive, with Moscow now the world's costliest city and also lacking decent hotel space. Tourist visitors to Russia fell 20 percent in 2005, although the now-liberated and newly affluent Russians are travelling the world in hitherto unheard-of numbers. Fluctuating tourist figures affect some countries much more than others. At least Russia has oil and natural gas to fall back on. Poor Bali, several of whose tourist haunts were struck by suicide bombings in 2002 and 2005, saw its visitor numbers plummet from 160,000 a year before the first bombing to virtually zero. Visitor numbers were just beginning to recover when the second bombing caused a 40 percent drop in visitors to the island. And unlike the Russians, the Balinese are almost totally reliant on international travellers for their livelihood.

Travel creates work. For every traveller, there seems to be three or four people whose income depends on that one person. And not just the obvious jobs – the travel agents, the pilots, the flight attendants, the taxi drivers, the hotel cleaners, the housemaids, the tour guides, the waitresses – but also the artisans, the craft market stall-holders, the souvenir sellers, the croupiers, the snack bar proprietors, the pamphlet printers, the pimps and the prostitutes. In tourist destinations that are popular with the elderly, like the Costa Brava, Honolulu, Florida or Surfer's Paradise, it's the pharmacists who do particularly well, a doctor told me. The over-70 travellers are forever forgetting, misplacing or losing their medication, he said, so they have to go to the local pharmacist for replacements. So whenever a tour party or cruise ship hoves into view, the pharmacists rub their hands together with glee, in expectation of hundreds of replacement medicines. Optometrists do very well too, evidently, from the misplaced or broken spectacles of the elderly.

To the locals everywhere, a foreign traveller is a walking wallet, a cash carrier who must somehow be parted from the prized currency he or she brings with them. In most places, but particularly in countries where resources are few, imaginative tactics are used to separate the tourists from their money.

On a tiny island in Melanesia I visited from a cruise ship, the locals had just a few hours to make as much profit as they could. Ships stopped there only three or four time a year, and the passengers would be on shore for eight hours at the most, so the islanders had limited time to put their entrepreneurial skills into practice. But with what ingenuity they went about it.

Set out for sale around the island was every conceivable item the islanders thought the passengers might want to buy: sarongs, carvings, spears, clubs, shells, brown dolls, plastic flowers, kava powder, drinking coconuts. For ten dollars European girls could get their hair braided and pretend they were Africans; for five dollars their fathers could join in a kava school with local men.

I wandered about the island, marvelling at these small examples of private enterprise. Just above the beach was a painted plywood cut-out of a mermaid, with a hole you could stick your face into and pretend to be one. Next to it was a similar opportunity for a career change, this time an image of a fearsome pirate; also with a hole where you could put your face. Making like a buccaneer in this part of the world, where kidnapping 'Blackbirders' wreaked tragedy in the nineteenth century, seemed to me to be 'culturally insensitive', but there were plenty of takers at five dollars a head. I also eschewed the communal kava bowl, which stood on a crate under a corrugated iron lean-to, not because I don't like kava, but because the bowl looked as if it would be a fertile nursery for the hepatitis B virus.

In the centre of the little island, under the coconut palms, I saw a hand-printed notice: 'Have Your Photo Taken with the Cannibals and the Cannibal Pot. "Welcome".' Nearby, atop a heap of driftwood, was a large, black, iron pot. Around its sides licked painted orange and red flames. A red and black sign declared it to be 'Cannibal Soup'.

Two local men, black-skinned and lithe with unruly hair and beards, dressed in flaring grass skirts and carrying spears, stood beside the mock pyre. The charge? Two dollars if the visitor was photographed standing outside the cannibal pot, five dollars if he sat inside it. Being an intrepid traveller, I opted for the inside location, and was photographed there by the cannibals' assistant – also semi-naked and with feral hair, although he was remarkably conversant with the workings of a digital camera – while the other two men bent close to me, snarled and held their machetes to my throat. Investigations revealed that the cannibals' cooking vessel had been a tri-pot, left on the island 40 years before, when the whaling station there closed down.

The exercise over I stepped out of the pot, paid the fee, shook hands with the grinning man-eaters and wandered on through the palms to the other side of the island. There, on a golden sand beach, the visitor could 'adopt' a tethered sea turtle for 30 dollars, then watch as the creature was liberated in the lagoon. One small turtle lay in a compound on the sand, its flippers moving feebly, looking very depressed. I watched as a family looked sorrowfully at the turtle and paid over the money. The young boy of the family carried the turtle down to the lagoon tenderly and released it there. For their compassion, the family received a certificate, signed by the chief of the island, endorsing their deed. But as I walked away I harboured the terrible suspicion that another local was waiting around the corner of the island to recapture the slow-swimming turtle and tether it again.

The ship weighed anchor and sailed away. I estimated that the 1200 passengers must have left at least $120,000 on the little island in the few hours they'd been ashore. Not bad pickings for the locals, of whom there were about a hundred. $120,000. Enough to buy not just many new jandals and disposable nappies, but petrol for the outboards, another fishing net, maybe a new generator and a second-hand truck. Almost enough to sustain the community until the next cruise ship called by in a few months' time.

Travel statistics are extreme whether they're global or local, none more so than those figures that pop up regularly in front of you on the screens in the aircraft cabin. You are now travelling, the screen informs you, at 805kph, or 500mph. That is fast. You're 11,582 metres, or 38,000 feet above the Earth. Much higher than the summit of Mount Everest. And the temperature just through the perspex window beside you is minus 49 degrees Celsius. That's very, very cold.

Enough statistics, let's get on with the trip.

# The Boy Traveller

Growing up in a small town in Taranaki gave me an early urge to travel. My home town was a very long way from anywhere else. In a collection of short stories I called the place 'The Town on the Edge of the World', because to me it seemed to be so far from the centre. From an early age I became aware that in that centre was a world vastly different and more exciting than my own. An avid reader, I had already discovered this other, exotic world through the town library, which became my skylight onto that world. Adventure stories set in historical Europe, frontier America, the streets of English cities and on tropical islands fired my imagination. Copies of *National Geographic*, with their colour plates of ancient Middle Eastern cities, terraced Asian rice paddies and bare-breasted Hottentots, captivated me. Such magazines and books transported me vicariously to regions far beyond my own, and as I grew older I yearned to see them for myself. Many other young New Zealanders must have experienced this inchoate wanderlust, a consequence of growing up in a country a very long way from anywhere else. Sharing no border with another country encourages the desire to see the infinite range of places beyond one's own shores.

It's likely that the impulse to wander has always been present in the human spirit. It was well over a million years ago when the first true humans, *Homo erectus*, packed up their stone axes and clubs and set out from East Africa to see what lay beyond the Rift Valley. In Bill Bryson's words, these hominids '... were unprecedentedly adventurous and spread across the globe with what seems to have been breathtaking rapidity'. Our earliest ancestors must have been great travellers, driven by an inherent desire to discover what lay over the next mountain range, plain or sea. That the descendants of these first travellers eventually ended up in places like the Algarve, Piedmont, Siberia, Java, Patagonia and Opunake is a tribute not only to their curiosity, but also their courage and endurance.

Yet once they had arrived somewhere accommodating, not all travellers felt the urge to keep going. For many people, their forebears' destination became the ultimate one. This was one of the first things I learned while on my own travels – that the need to wander on is not necessarily universal. I found this out firstly when I needed to ask directions while travelling in a country which was new to me. Often my inquiries as to the way to the village or town I sought would be met by incomprehension or a nonplussed shrug, even if the destination turned out to be just a few kilometres down the road. Or around the street corner, as happened once in London. In spite of the allure of 'abroad', the phenomenon of mass travel and the actuality of the global village, it seems that a surprisingly large number of modern humans, *Homo sapiens*, are content to not stray far from their own territory.

Once while touring Devon, England, I went for an early morning walk. Coming upon a local farmhand leaning on a gate, a man of about 50, I struck up a conversation with him. He was an amiable, ruddy-faced rustic with a wonderful local accent, all 'oys' and 'ahs' and 'yerrs'. Detecting that I wasn't from 'roun' ear', he asked where it was that I was from.

'New Zealand,' I replied. There was a very long silence while the man absorbed the implications of this. Then, scratching hard at his face stubble, he said slowly, 'New Zealand …' Staring into the distance, he said dreamily, 'I wen' to Plymouth, once.'

But for me, distance has always lent enchantment, a perceived attraction enhanced by travellers' stories. During my boyhood, first-hand accounts of these were usually provided by my parents' friends – illustrated with colour slides of indifferent quality – upon their return from places like Fiji, Australia and Norfolk Island, the most popular destinations for people from my home town. My parents, small town people to the core and not greatly interested in 'overseas', did not venture off-shore until they were well into their 50s. Judging from their relief to be home again, they found it an earth-shattering experience.

When I was sixteen I read my first travel book. Written by an Australian called Colin Simpson, it was the account of the author's journeys through Europe; from Iberia to Scandinavia. Published in hardback and illustrated with full colour plates, the book was devoured by its young reader. In it Mr Simpson described ancient cathedrals, quaint canal boats, cobbled streets and medieval castles. His book contained photographs of peasant farmers harvesting corn, happy day-trippers on cross-channel ferries and beautiful Scandinavian girls with their faces upturned blissfully to the mid-summer sun. I found the book irresistible. To me these scenes and peoples held so much more appeal than the share-milkers, cow paddocks, barbed wire fences and unsightly buildings of my own world. There were no castles or cobblestones in Opunake, although there were plenty of peasant farmers. Reading Colin Simpson whetted my appetite for the world. I could hardly wait to get out and see Europe for myself. Once there, I promised myself, I too would throw a torch beam onto Neolithic cave paintings in France, swallow pickled herrings at a canal-side café in Amsterdam, travel on a ferry across the Kategatt, drink Pilsener in a cobbled square in Prague and meet a flaxen-haired Scandinavian girl who tilted her face skyward like a sunflower.

It was not merely the content of the Colin Simpson book that stirred me, but the realisation *that this man doesn't just travel to places, he travels to places and writes about them for a living.* This seemed to me to be such a wonderful concept, such a blissful occupation, that it seemed too good to be true. Yet it was true, he did it. I read all his other books, the ones set in the South Pacific and Asia. *This was what a travel writer did.* I resolved that one day I would do it too. It took me another 25 years, but eventually I did it. But first, I had to travel.

I chose Asia first, because I studied the region at university. At the age of 26, though, the closest I had been to the East was Wellington's Oriental Bay. Fired with enthusiasm, I planned my Eastern itinerary. Having selected various destinations, I read about them assiduously, noting what I would do when I got there. I would climb a live volcano in Java, gaze at the Taj Mahal in Delhi and ride the tram to the Peak on Hong Kong Island. Dressed in native garb, I would immerse myself in the streets of Jakarta, New Delhi and Kowloon, carefully noting the sights, sounds and fragrances that surrounded me.

World, here I come.

⌒

Nothing had prepared me for the realities: the squalor, the degradation, the decay, the teeming millions and their stench.

Especially the stench. My first stop was Jakarta, a nightmarish city of filth, shanties and stenches emanating from its wretched slums and disease-ridden canals. Instead of climbing a live volcano I holed up in the Hyatt Hotel, Jakarta, too terrified to venture into the streets in case I was infected, assaulted or murdered, until I could fly out again. From there I went to New Delhi. Again, heaving crowds of importuning locals assailed me. At the airport, children punched and scratched each other for the privilege of carrying my bag from the concourse to a taxi; in my hotel the lift attendant lived in the lift and the toilet cleaner lived in the toilet. In the street, suppurating stumps were thrust under my nose. Again, my hotel became my haven, but it was cavernous and gloomy, ornately decorated with red velvet drapes, reminding me of my grandmother's house. Indian music was piped through all the rooms, 24 hours a day, except that to my ears it wasn't music, it was more like the sound cats make when they are being strangled. I left for Hong Kong, leaving behind the squeezed cat music, the limbless beggars and the soiled streets.

This was the world? Get me out of it.

In Hong Kong I at least felt safe, even in the teeming tenements and markets of Kowloon. The people seemed too busy to be threatening, although I was dextrously relieved of most of my travel funds by a nineteen-year-old Cantonese conman who was too considerate of my needs to be true. But at least I felt I could venture from my hotel and explore the sweaty streets, at least I was trying to come to terms with an exotic destination. Then, one hot evening, I ate out.

Kowloon's narrow streets were a jumble of neon signs, shop-houses, rickshaws and delivery vehicles. The shops and streets carried comical names like Fat Man Lam, Wong Hen, Wo Hop, Tin Kan, Won Shek, Li Kee Kok, Long Kok, Long Fuk and King Fuk. Wet washing attached to the end of bamboo poles dripped down onto me as I pushed my way through the crowds, my nostrils filled with the stink of decaying vegetables, human sweat, boiled noodles, and the grease from bits of pig and glazed ducks that rotated slowly on spits in eatery windows. And it was in one of these little cafés that I ate my first meal away from my rabbit warren of a hotel, where previously I had stuck resolutely to sausages, bacon, eggs and toast.

There were about eight small tables in the place, each covered with oil cloth. The floor was covered with cracked linoleum and a ceiling fan churned away ineffectually at the sweltering air. Sagging red lanterns, like decrepit concertinas, dangled from the ceiling around the fan; a few fly-spotted prints of Chinese landscapes hung on the walls. From behind a bead curtain came a banging of pans, the cries of cooks and the reek of boiling oil. But the place was cheap, and I was now running out of money, thanks to the tailored suit I had been talked into buying by the Cantonese conman.

I took a seat at one of the tables, then looked at the plastic-jacketed menu. It was written in Cantonese and English. The ingredients were certainly different: ducks' feet soup, pickled pigs' intestines, stewed chicken necks. The waiter, whom I assumed was also the owner, was a short fat man wearing a black apron over his shorts and singlet. Balding and with a waxen complexion, he watched me closely as I studied the menu. I opted for the only dish with which I was in any way familiar: chicken chow mein. The man went through the bead curtain, there was more shouting and banging of pots, a hissing of steam, then a few minutes later he re-emerged, carrying a heaped, steaming plate of white meat and vegetables.

Very hungry by now, I sprinkled some soy sauce over the pile of food, then attacked it with the supplied fork, knowing I couldn't cope with the chopsticks which were also provided. The vegetables on the plate – principally sliced cabbage, broccoli and carrots – were tasty enough, but the pieces of chicken atop the heap began to trouble me. Like the vegetables, the meat had been sliced, but it bore no resemblance to any part of a chicken that I had ever seen before. Most of the meat was in small rings, surrounding a central bone, rather like segments of a miniature ox tail. The meat was also rather gristly. Wondering what breed of Chinese chicken could have produced a tail, I ate on determinedly, sucking the meat from each piece of bone, then placing the bones on the edge of the plate.

Then, gradually, I became aware that I was being observed. Looking over at the curtain, I saw several small children peeping around the door at me, along with the stout man and a similarly shaped woman. Trying to ignore the spectators, I continued with my eating. But why, I wondered as I ate, are they taking such an interest in me and my meal? And as I stared at the remaining portions of chicken, an appalling realisation dawned: they are watching the Westerner eat chicken because it isn't chicken. It's…it's…it can only be the tail of … *dog* …or perhaps … *cat* … I began to gag.

Now, however, I also had a pride attack. Suspecting that the peering family wanted to see if I was brave enough to finish their disgusting fare, I decided that there would be no retreat. I would eat every scrap of it. And I did, except for the little round tail bones that were lined up carefully on the side of my plate. On completion of the meal, I wiped my mouth on the paper towel supplied, left the requisite number of Hong Kong dollars in the saucer on the table and nodded triumphantly at the big-eyed faces still peering around the kitchen door. Then I walked out of the scummy little restaurant, down the crowded street and vomited into the first alleyway I came to.

I had a long way to go.

# The Writing Traveller

Twenty-five years had passed since I first dreamed of becoming a travel writer. I had seen something of the world, especially Europe and Asia, and I had written about it. Now I was back in my home region, now I was a travel writer. It was a vocation, but it was by no means as straightforward a vocation as I had imagined it to be, all those years ago when I was a boy. Others were traversing the same territory.

Paul Theroux. The man haunted me. He was the spectre at my back, the phantom of my opera. Wherever I went, he had been; whatever I saw, he had seen. And written about it already.

Shortly before my first travel book, *Passages – Journeys in Polynesia*, was published, Paul Theroux's *The Happy Isles of Oceania* appeared. I had no idea that he was also researching and writing a book about the islands of the Pacific, but having enjoyed Theroux's earlier travel accounts, particularly his journeys by rail through China and India, and because his new book was set in the same region as mine, I read *The Happy Isles* with great interest.

A thorough curmudgeon with an outsized ego, Theroux

nevertheless managed to extract some humour from his wide-ranging journeys through the Pacific. His travels were lent elements of self-inflicted hardship through his habit of paddling a collapsible kayak around the islands in the absence of his preferred form of transport, trains. *The Happy Isles* also had a New Zealand connection in that Theroux at one stage teamed up with David Lange on Aitutaki, Lange's favourite Cook Island. He went on to dine with the then-Governor-General of New Zealand, Dame Catherine Tizard, in Fiji and described in unpleasant detail her eating habits, a description which Dame Cath later strongly denied. Like Theroux's other travel books, *The Happy Isles* made entertaining reading, although its tone was largely negative. The title is ironic, though – Theroux found it difficult to write anything positive about Oceania. As such, it contrasted markedly with my journeys through Polynesia, in which I did my best to look on the bright side.

So, coincidentally, two travel books set in the South Pacific had appeared at roughly the same time. Naturally, in view of its author's fame and some controversial content, *The Happy Isles* attracted considerable publicity and strong sales, and the Theroux publicity pot was still bubbling when *Passages* was published some months later. Surprising to me, comparisons were drawn between the two books. Local reviewers seized upon the similarity in subject matter and sized the books up against each other, contrasting their respective styles, their angles, the coverage and even, in one instance, the probable incomes of the two authors (dramatic contrast there, the reviewer rightly guessed. I'll bet Paul never has to carry cases full of unsold books when he travels).

Then, in the course of writing further South Pacific stories, I made several more journeys into Oceania, mainly to the Cook Islands and French Polynesia. And everywhere I went, people had either read *The Happy Isles*, or met Paul Theroux, or sometimes both. I became accustomed, whenever I mentioned my job, to people nodding and responding, 'Ah …like Paul Theroux.' The man had certainly put himself about. Even on tiny islands with minimal facilities, somebody would tell me, 'He was here, you know, Paul Theroux. Paddling his kayak. Then he went home and wrote nasty things about us.'

His book and its author polarised readers. Around a table in a Rarotonga restaurant, two good friends yelled at each other and almost came to blows over *The Happy Isles*. One saw him as a literary carpetbagger and a 'smart-ass', the other regarding his writing as refreshingly cynical, a welcome antidote to the usual Pacific brochure clichés. These two readers pretty much summed up the divergent opinions about Paul Theroux the travel writer.

It was in the Marquesas Islands, remote and geographically spectacular, that I found the spoor of Paul Theroux to be freshest. He had gone to the Marquesas on the inter-island vessel *Moana Nui* via the Tuamotus, and *The Happy Isles* gives good coverage to this part of his journeys through Oceania. And one night, on the remote, rugged island of Nuku Hiva, I gained some insight into the renowned travel writer's technique.

The Keikahanui Inn is perched high up at one end of the spectacular bay of Taiahoe, a huge horseshoe-shaped indentation in the coastline of Nuku Hiva. Sheltered from almost all winds, Taiahoe Bay is a popular port-of-call for yachts sailing from California to Tahiti and places further south. I wasn't staying at the Keikahanui Inn, but I called in there one evening to have a drink with Jean Marie, an alcoholic Frenchman I had met in the village, who was the resident chef.

As I was having a Hinano lager with Jean Marie, the inn manager came and joined us. A Californian, Rose Corser has lived on Nuku Hiva for many years and is now a widow. Rose's inn consists of several bungalows and a restaurant, all of which enjoy panoramic views through the tropical trees and over the bay. Rose is frail, but dignified and courteous in the way of very civilised Americans. I mentioned to her that I was here to write about the Marquesas. Rose looked thoughtful.

'So you're a travel writer?'

'Mmm.'

'Like Paul Theroux.'

'Well…' I gave her what by now was a practised disclaimer. Rose nodded.

'He stayed here.' Her tone was dry. 'In one of my bungalows.'

'Really?'

'Oh yes. He talked to me for a long time, about this island, about the archaeological remains in the valleys, about Herman Melville.'

(Melville's novel *Typee* (1846) was inspired by the writer's experiences as a ship's deserter on Nuku Hiva.)

Remembering that Rose had lived on the island for a long time, I said, 'Theroux must have found you to be a good source of information.'

Her face clouded over. 'Oh, sure. But did you read what he wrote about me?'

I shook my head. I had, but I couldn't recall it. Rose went out to the back of the restaurant and returned with a copy of *The Happy Isles*. She found the section on Nuku Hiva, then read aloud from it in her well-modulated voice.

'All canned goods were luxuries in the Marquesas. The people grew breadfruit and mangoes, and they caught fish. If they had spare money they treated themselves to a can of Spam or one of the crunchy snacks they like so much.' Rose paused, then continued. 'Now get this: *"A girl might work as a waitress simply to be able to buy cigarettes,"* Rose Corson told me. *"At five dollars a pack the cigarettes would take most of her salary."*'

'All our discussions about Marquesan history and culture, and that's all he put in his book.' Rose closed the book ruefully. 'And he didn't even get my name right.'

This led me to wonder. How much else did Paul get wrong in *The Happy Isles*?

Paul the intrepid traveller made it to the Taipivai Valley, east of Taiahoe, the valley that Melville depicted in *Typee*. I was writing a piece on Melville, so naturally I went there too. It is a place of great beauty, isolated from Nuku Hiva's other bays. A small river runs down the valley, past breadfruit trees, banana palms and village houses.

The valley in Melville's novel features a large lake, across which he sailed with the lovely Typee princess, Fayaway. There is no real lake in Taipivai; only a small, but pretty backwater where the river debouches into an inlet. Theroux was affronted by this ('another illusion was shattered', he writes sourly), an astonishing reaction from a man who is also a novelist. Did he not appreciate that Melville was a writer of fiction? That *Typee* was largely the product of his imagination?

So it went on. By my journey's end I had become hardened to the comment, usually from Americans, 'Oh, a writer. Like Paul Theroux.' It was too difficult to explain, so I would just reply, 'Something like that.'

I didn't paddle a kayak, I didn't have an audience with the King of Tonga, I didn't come across David Lange on Aitutaki. Theroux did all of these things, and more. I did have a meal with Sir Geoffrey Henry, the-then Prime Minister of the Cook Islands, though. His eating habits, alas, were impeccable.

And on Rarotonga I did manage to find something that Paul didn't, a locomotive. A local eccentric and train lover imported it, from Poland of all places, and is lovingly restoring it. As I looked at the as-yet trackless engine, which will eventually be running on the island, I was seized with the notion of a Theroux-type travel book to which I will beat Paul. A title springs to mind: *Great Train Journeys of Rarotonga*.

Paul Theroux's flaw as a travel writer, it seems to me, is to make the mistake of placing himself at the centre of his journeys. Too often Paul becomes more important than his destination.

There is, unavoidably, a large element of self in the travel-writing genre – the writer must from the outset have a somewhat inflated ego to think that others will be interested in what he writes of his experiences – but as with journalism in general, if the 'I' is paramount, the writing will seldom be memorable. A writer as skilful as Bill Bryson can get away with placing himself upstage, mainly because he has the additional quality of being able to create comic situations which allow the reader to forgive him for it. Bryson is agreeably self-deprecating; Theroux is disagreeably self-centred.

Always, travel writers must tread a delicate line between informing and entertaining their readers. Too much information and the writing becomes tedious; too much entertainment and the work draws accusations of frivolity. Some of the best travel writing has at its heart a personal quest, a search for something significant – an ancestral connection perhaps, or a site of historic provenance. And as with fiction writing, there must also be an element of drama to add tension to the story. Some of the most memorable travel writing comes from the school of what one connoisseur calls 'the Englishman abroad hopelessly out of his depth'.

One of the best exponents of this school is Jonathan Raban, who relishes putting himself into extreme circumstances – going down the Mississippi in a small boat, circumnavigating Britain as a novice sailor, sailing along the rugged west coast of North America – then reporting on the experience in a style that keeps readers on the edge of their seats. Raban is a brave man, as well as a gifted writer.

A fertile imagination is also required, to embellish the journey and depict its characters vividly. So it is unsurprising that the best travel writers – from Charles Dickens, Robert Louis Stevenson and Mark Twain onwards to Edith Warton, Martha Gellhorn, Anais Nin, Evelyn Waugh, Graham Greene, Bruce Chatwin and Pico Iyer – were (or are) novelists as well. Writers like these have made travel writing an honourable genre.

꒲

Today, however, just as travel has become a mass activity, so too has writing about it. Travel writing is now one of the most popular of literary genres, with the shelves of bookshops crammed with what is usually categorised as 'Armchair Travel'. If it sometimes seems that half the world is travelling, then it also seems that the other half has just gone home and written about it. Guide books too have proliferated, as travel itself has undergone explosive growth. One of the most familiar sights when travelling anywhere in the world is the 20-something backpacker, on a bus, a plane, at a café or beside the road, head buried in the pages of their bright blue bible, a Lonely Planet guide (650 titles published in 118 countries, annual sales of over six million). Lonely Planet is indisputably a publishing phenomenon, their guides crammed with useful information. I use them too. But if you're looking for peace, quiet and fair prices, stay away from any establishment recommended in one of these guides. Like its antecedent of the 1960s and '70s, the Frommer Guides such as *Europe on $10 a Day* (sic) – whose accommodation and 'sights to see' recommendations were invariably followed by inundations of travellers and the subsequent exploitation of them by locals.

A guide book is not a travel book, however. The former should always be empirical, the latter is personal and impressionistic. And with the market awash with travel books, the would-be travel author has had to resort to more and more unusual journeys to make publishers sit up and take notice of their accomplishments. People write about such feats as riding a tandem bicycle through the Himalayas, circumnavigating the world solo, riding a horse across Mongolia, traversing the Indian sub-continent on an elephant, climbing Mt Everest on artificial legs, cycling from one side of Australia to the other, going along the Great Wall of China in a wheelchair, or swimming up the Thames from the North Sea to its source. Much travel writing is testimony to the degree of suffering which obsessive travellers are prepared to inflict upon themselves.

There is no finer contemporary example of the 'hardship school' of travel writing than the American writer Eric Hansen (*Motoring with Mohammed* and *Bird Man and the Lap Dancer*). He goes to places where there are only nomadic hunters and gatherers, he searches for the remains of a crashed aircraft's deceased passengers in the jungles of Kalimantan, he camps out with Bedouin in Saudi Arabia, he eats bee larvae soup and smoked camel intestines on the side of the road in Yemen. He is, indisputably, a fully paid-up member of the intrepid travel writing school. Eric, with whom I once appeared on a travel writers' panel, is not the slightest bit interested in luxury travel because, he told me, it's 'isolating, precious and boring'.

This can be true, but often isn't. I know, because I belong firmly to the opposite school of travel writing, what might be called the 'craven school'. I've never been on a camel or a yak, and I don't intend to. I keep away from places where there are insurrections or plagues. Jungles I find too wet and too impenetrable. I eat only recognisable food in reputable restaurants. I fly in business class whenever it's offered and I love it when I spot someone clutching a notice with my name on it after I've emerged nervously into the arrivals hall. I like comfortable beds in well-appointed hotel rooms, a pristine white towelling dressing gown in the wardrobe and the BBC News channel on the television.

To avoid Eric's accusation that such travel is isolating, precious and boring, by day I boldly venture out from my hotel to enjoy mild adventures. I climb only low mountains and kayak only in still, warm lagoons. My preferred mode of transport (provided the terrain isn't too hilly) is a bicycle, not a camel, because bikes don't bite; also you can go fast enough to cover plenty of ground, yet slow enough to absorb the sights and smells along the way. I have made long transfers to airports in the early hours of the morning on remote islands by bicycle, with my heavy luggage and cartons of unsold books perched precariously on the handlebars. To me this is adventure.

Some readers of travel literature welcome the trend to intrepidness, however, as it spares them the discomfort of extreme travel while still enabling them to experience it, albeit vicariously. To quote poet Kevin Ireland again: 'There seems to me only one answer to the problem that mass travel has created, increasing international contempt, hatred and tension. That is, leave travel to intrepid adventurers, and preferably ones who can write well, so that they can bring back reports on the exotic places they have been to, the extraordinary incidents they have witnessed, and the delightful and interesting people they have come across. If you can't do it alone, then the next best thing is the old-fashioned way: do it through the pages of a good book.'

One of the finest twentieth-century travel writers is one who is also among the least-lauded; Englishman Norman Lewis (1908–2003). A shy, modest man, Lewis travelled before he turned writer, going first to Spain in the early 1930s. By the time he was in his mid-20s he was interested in nothing else but travelling and writing. He spent the next 60 years of his life observing, as one of his obituarists noted, 'the ebb and flow of governments, the dissolution of indigenous tribal cultures and the activities of missionaries, bandits, profiteers and political scene-shifters'. Lewis wrote memorably about Amazonia, Arabia, Indo-China, Sicily and Spain. In *A Dragon Apparent* (1951), he wrote: 'On the morning of the fourth day the dawn light daubed our faces as we came down the skies of Cochin-China ... with engines throttled back, the plane dropped from sur-alpine heights in a tremorless glide, settling in the new, morning air of the plains like a dragonfly on the surface of a calm lake.'

Wherever he went, one critic observed, 'His concern to

uncover human comedy and calamity was the same'. This concern is no more apparent than in his book *An Empire of the East*. In it Norman Lewis writes about the extremes of the sprawling island nation of Indonesia, from Aceh in the west of Sumatra to the rainforests and the world's highest gold mine, in Papua in the east, in a manner which makes his accounts unforgettable. He ventures without a trace of fear or self-pity into malarial swamps, cloud-piercing mountains and war-tormented landscapes, revealing as he does more about Indonesia than anything else I have ever read. I came to the end of this story filled with admiration for the writer's courage and fortitude. It was only later that I was startled to realise that *An Empire of the East*, published in 1993, was researched and written when Norman Lewis was 84 years old. I had read of Lewis's self-effacement, and there could be no greater testimony to this quality than his writing itself. There is no perpetual 'I-I-I-I' in Norman Lewis's travel writing. Like Eric Newby, like Bruce Chatwin, Norman Lewis raised travel writing to an art form.

∽

It's unlikely, too, that these travel writers ever accepted a free trip anywhere.

Today, however, established travel writers are commonly offered free airfares and accommodation in exchange for publicising in the travel pages of magazines or newspapers the destination to which they have been sent. (Sometimes, on newspapers and magazines, these free trips are allocated to office staff, not necessarily qualified writers, causing rancorous reactions from those not chosen.) Professional travel writers can be sent to a selected destination by travel authorities, public relations companies or the publication in which the story will appear. This raises a question of ethics. Having been provided with gratis airfares, transfers and accommodation, is the travel writer obliged to write a glowing account of the destination? Must the writer always bear in mind that those would-be travellers who will read his or her story will actually have to pay for what the writer has been presented with? What happens if the destination turns out to be considerably less than the writer's expectations? Can the writer be seen to be compromising personal principles and professional by extolling a place that is in reality horrid?

Here are two stories pertinent to these significant questions.

The catamaran *Haumana* glided across the lagoon of Raiatea. She carried 20 passengers, ten crew, and was modern and extremely comfortable. My cabin in the bow of the vessel was air-conditioned. There was also a TV set and a DVD player, but who could be bothered watching while the real world alongside was so lovely? We were cruising on *Haumana* through the waters of the Leeward Islands, in the Society Group, north-west of Tahiti. The vessel's draft was so shallow that her Tahitian skipper could nudge her bow up onto a sandbank so that we could disembark in the shallows without using the tender. By day the weather was fine, the sky enamel blue, the 30°C temperatures moderated by the trade wind that blew over the islands from the south-east. By day we cruised the sea between the islands, in the late afternoons we entered one of the lagoons. There, as the sun descended to the horizon then slipped beneath it, the Pacific sky flared orange and red. On the upper deck of *Haumana* I sipped cold Hinano lager and chatted to my fellow passengers, from Italy, the States and Germany, then went down to the dining room and ate a four-course dinner prepared by the ship's French chef. Afterwards we returned to the upper deck where we enjoyed liqueurs under the stars, then I retired to my cabin and made notes for my story, accompanied by the soft slosh of lagoon water against *Haumana*'s twin hulls. This was blissful enough, but there was more to come.

On the third day we went through the pass of Bora Bora and entered the lagoon from which the massif central of the island, Otemanu, rose up sheer like a great green tusk. The waters of the lagoon were variegated shades of green and blue, intensely green and blue, so bright they dazzled. On the outer edge, long rows of palm trees lined the motus – attenuated islets of coral rock – surrounding the lagoon. The air was hot and dry, and on the horizon were the shadowy profiles of other islands, their peaks swathed in cotton cloud.

*Haumana* slowed, then stopped, in the middle of the lagoon. 'What's up?' I asked Tomita, our transvestite maitre d'h. 'Oh, we stop 'ere to pick up some more passengers. They arrive on the flight from Papeete.'

The ship's inflatable tender was put into the water where it powered off towards the airport, located on one of the island's motus. Minutes later the tender was back alongside *Haumana* and our four additional passengers were climbing aboard.

There was Simone, who was French, originally from Normandy; Hinana, part-Tahitian and part-Spanish, from Papeete; Valentine, part-Chinese and part-Spanish, from Moorea; and Vaiana, part-French and part-Madagascan, from Noumea. All in their early 20s, they were university graduates, training for careers in the 'hospitality industry' and the cruise on *Haumana* was part of their training. Between them they spoke fluent French, Spanish, Cantonese, Tahitian and English. And miscegenation having worked its hereditary magic, they were all beautiful.

For the next two days we cruised around Bora Bora. We called at the harbour of the capital town, Vaitape, to shop at its market and eat at its snack bars; we stopped at the island's motus, swam and had picnic lunches under their palm trees. Simone and Hinana and Valentine and Vaiana put on their bikinis, frolicked and swam in the lagoon, then stretched out in the sun to dry under the palms. Impure thoughts entered my mind. The young women were all articulate, sophisticated and well read, they had French flair, their conversations and laughter filled the ship. We had long discussions on the deck and over dinner, and by the time the cruise came to an end I was very fond of them. When we made our farewells at the airport each one kissed me gently on both cheeks and murmured 'Au revoir, Gray-em,'; the fragrance of frangipani blossom and coconut oil clung about their hair like a heavenly bouquet.

Back in Papeete, my Tahitian-French friend Lola smiled knowingly and said, 'How did you enjoy the cruise on *Haumana*?'

'It was wonderful,' I replied.

'So you will write nice things about it?'

'I will.'

Lola nodded with satisfaction. 'That's good.' She picked up a sheet of paper. 'Now, you know you always wanted to go to the Austral Islands?'

'Yes.' These are French Polynesia's southernmost islands. No one I knew had ever been there. I certainly hadn't. And neither had Lola. She gave me another little smile.

'I 'ave arranged for you to go there. To Rurutu, for four days. To write a story.' She gave me a quizzical look. 'Can you go? This afternoon?'

'I can.'

Watching Rurutu appear beneath the plane, I shivered with anticipation. There was a wave-tossed reef, a lagoon, a rocky coastline, a narrow coastal plain and a rugged interior. Again I felt the thrill of having a new island to explore, and write about. You could watch migrating whales from the shore here, I'd been told. And there were marvellous limestone caves in the island's interior.

Two days later, I sat on the beach below my hotel, a writing pad on my knee. The narrow stretch of rubbly beach was littered with broken furniture – irreparable plastic chairs and tables. Discarded plastic water bottles lay everywhere. Earlier that day I had had an altercation with the hotel director, a surly Frenchman who sat in his office from morning till night, smoking and watching cartoons on TV. The argument was about the whales. I had told him I wanted to see the whales. M'sieur Le Director dragged on his Gauloise.

'The whales 'ave gone.'

'Gone? Where?'

'I doan know.' He shrugged. 'Where do whales go?'

'Will they come back?'

'How would I know? I doan know anything about whales.'

He shrugged again, then walked away, before I could hit him.

That exchange followed my trip to the caves, where I was taken by the director's wife, a sulky, toothless Tahitian woman. She drove me along the coast in total silence, turned up a side road, stopped at the end, nodded up ahead and muttered, 'La caverne.'

I got out. There was a large cavern, from the roof of which hung a few stalactites. They had been sprayed with red graffiti, in French. A tunnel led off from one side of the cave. 'Can I go down that tunnel?'

The directrice shook her head. 'You need a guide.'

'Can you guide me?'

'Non.'

'So that's it? That's your cave?'

She flicked up her eyebrows disdainfully, in a gesture that effectively said that's it. Take it or leave it.

As she drove me back to the hotel, I fumed. I could live with the fact that the hotel was a dump – the swimming pool was malarial, my room dirty and with every fixture broken or malfunctioning – but I couldn't stand the insufferable rudeness from the manager and his wife. They made Sybil and Basil Fawlty seem like Mother and Father Teresa. And now that the whales had buggered off – and who could blame them? – the island itself had absolutely nothing to offer. The lagoon was filled with razor-sharp rocks and the district around the hotel was infested with diseased, aggressive dogs. When I tried to cycle around Rurutu I got no further than 50 metres down the road before a pack of the dogs launched themselves at me and began snapping at my legs. I tried riding with one hand and striking out at them with a heavy stick held in the other, but the dogs sent for reinforcements and they became too many to fend off.

I tried to walk along the beach instead, but in one direction it was completely blocked by a rugged bluff, and the other way by the end of the airport runway. Here, sitting on the sand beneath a windsock that drooped like a used condom, was a group of local youths. Dark-faced, bare-footed, dressed in grubby singlets and jeans, they all wore their baseball caps back to front. On the ground beside them was a large CD player blasting out gangsta rap. As I approached, intending to walk around them, they eyed me with undisguised hostility. I saw them begin to mutter among themselves. *They're planning to assault and rob me,* I thought, *and there's nothing I can do about it.* Yes, I can, I told myself, I can turn around and go back. And taking a deep breath, I did just that. Walking carefully, attempting nonchalance, I saw a chunk of driftwood land on the sand beside me, and heard an aggressive shout. I kept walking, back to my accommodation.

So there I was, confined to the dismal hotel. It was like being under house arrest. Had there been interesting guests for me to talk to, this would not have mattered so much, but the only other people staying there was a French couple with two young children who looked as miserable as I felt. And we couldn't leave early because the only plane out wasn't leaving for three days. We were all trapped.

I had been sent here to Rurutu to write a story, preferably one extolling the place. But there was absolutely nothing positive that I could write. The island had no attractions and was almost as repellent as the hotel. Sitting on the littered sand, I picked up a broken chair leg and hurled it into the lagoon. Then I thought again. Yes, there was. I *could* write something. And I did. For the remainder of my time on Rurutu I sat on the beach and composed a letter to the tourism authorities in Papeete, writing it first in English, then with the aid of my dictionary translating it laboriously into French for the authorities. While trying to maintain a degree of courtesy, I held nothing back. In summary, I wrote that the hotel was a disgrace, that it was in need of total refurbishment, starting with the director and directrice. I itemised its shortcomings, and the instances of rudeness I had had to put up with. 'And this,' I concluded, 'is all I will be writing about Rurutu.'

Lola read the report. She frowned; she pouted. 'This is terrible,' she said.

'I know,' I replied. 'And it needs to be read by someone who can do something about it.'

It was. Two days later, a government tourism representative flew to the island to inspect the hotel. And shortly afterwards, it was closed down. By the government. It was the oddest travel story I ever wrote.

That is another aspect of global travel – its unpredictability. No matter how careful the planning has been, how set the assumptions are, there are always surprises to be had in unfamiliar lands. Some are pleasant, many are not.

It was my first visit to South America, the first time I had been to the sprawling metropolis of Buenos Aires. My wife Gillian, our 22-year-old son Benjamin and I were staying in a hotel in the very centre of the city, on the 20-lane-wide Avenida 9 de Julio. We were finding the city to be as colourful, cosmopolitan and sophisticated as any in Europe. In fact given Buenos Aires' cafés, boutiques, street markets, opera house, leafy parks and ubiquitous heroic statuary, we could have been in Milan or Paris or Madrid. A large Italian influence was unexpected, but delightfully so, while tango dancers performing their seductive routines in the streets and parks were reminders that we were in the very heart of Latin America. The district of Recoleta was just a few minutes away from the hotel by taxi. A lively complex of cafés, restaurants, shops, art galleries and artisan stalls, Recoleta also has a fascinating cemetery, a necropolis whose ornate marble mausoleums house the remains of many once-prominent Argentinians, including Eva Peron. On the grass and under trees, couples danced the tango to live or recorded music, the women svelte, dark-eyed and enchanting, their male partners looking to me oily and lecherous.

Our hotel was oldish but comfortable; several storeys high, with a swimming pool on the roof. From this top level we could see that the city – built on almost entirely level land – reached to the horizon in every direction, its sprawl overlaid with a pale brown haze. Buenos Aires is home to 12,500,000 people. It was mid-summer, the air was hot and very dry. Refreshed after our roof-top swim, Benjamin and I got into the lift to return to our room on the fourth floor.

After the lift stopped at the sixth floor, a family of three got in, a man and a woman in their late 20s, and a little boy of about seven. Benjamin, who was learning Spanish, greeted them. 'Buenos dias,' he said. The father and mother smiled shyly and returned the greeting, both murmuring, 'Buenos dias', 'Buenos dias.' As the lift continued its slow descent, I studied the family surreptitiously. They were, to my delight, Andean Indians, the only ones we had so far seen in Argentina. I had read enough of Argentinian history to know that the story of the indigenous people here was an unhappy one; the few that had been living on the pampas when the Spanish colonised the land in the sixteenth century quickly succumbed to European disease and firearms. The 'Indians' of Argentina had virtually been exterminated.

But here, sharing our lift, was a family of authentic South American Indians. The husband and wife were both quite short, the husband slim, the wife dumpy. Both had dark skin, coal-black glossy hair and the high cheekbones of their race. The man's hair was cut short, the woman's hung in two braids over the front of her shoulders. She wore a colourful poncho around her shoulders, a black bowler hat and a long, flaring dress of coarse wool; her husband wore a multi-coloured jerkin over his shirt; their son a similar jacket and long black trousers. Both adults held their hands together in front of them, and I could see their worn fingers and blackened nails. The man wore an Andean-patterned, woollen hat, but incongruously, all three were also wearing white, new-looking Western-style sneakers. They lacked only nose flutes hanging from their belts to convey the very personification of the indigenous people of this continent.

My imagination was fired. This deracinated family had probably taken the long journey from the shores of Lake Titicaca, catching a train from La Paz to Cochabamba, then across the high plains of eastern Bolivia and right across Paraguay and into Argentina, carrying all their belongings in three battered suitcases before eventually arriving in Buenos Aires, where they would make a new life, playing traditional Andean tunes on their nose flutes in the city markets. My heart went out to them. How brave, I thought, to migrate from the Altiplano to this huge city to give their little boy the chance of a better existence than a lifetime of cutting rushes on the shores of Lake Titicaca, trying to grow potatoes in the stony soils of an intermontane Andean basin, gnawing coca against the cold. This family, it seemed to me, was on the way to embodying a small triumph of the human spirit.

The lift continued its slow decent. Benjamin and I spoke to each other about our plans for the rest of the day. As we did so, I saw the man and the woman glancing at us, curiously. The little boy stared up at us with an impish grin. Then the man put his hand to his mouth, gave an apologetic little cough and said in careful English, 'Excuse me. Where do you come from?'

I replied, slowly and with equal care, 'Nueva Zelandia.' Then I repeated, 'Auck-land. In Nueva Zelandia.'

The man's face erupted with delight. In a marked Kiwi accent, he said, 'We're from Point Chev. Whereabouts in Auckland do you live?'

Originally from Peru, they had indeed left their home country in search of a better life, but in New Zealand, not Argentina. After immigrating to New Zealand in 2000, the husband and wife had both taken work as commercial cleaners in central Auckland. Their little boy, Carlos, went to school in Point Chevalier, Auckland. He spoke good English and was doing well at gymnastics. They had returned to Peru to attend a family wedding in Lima – hence the traditional-style clothes – and had flown to Buenos Aires the day before to connect with the Aerolinas Argentina flight back to Auckland. It turned out that we were on the same flight home, three days later. We chatted again during a refuelling stopover in Rio Gallegos, in southern Argentina, and during the flight Carlos entertained the entire economy class cabin with his antics, specialising in doing backward flips in the aisle – a typical Kiwi kid.

# Maps and the Traveller

A map is the world writ small. A good map is as indispensable to the conscientious traveller as a book of recipes is to an aspiring cook. Literal and sometimes figurative representations of the Earth's surface, maps can also be works of art, syntheses of form and function. A judicious application of colour to a map clarifies and enhances landscapes. Maps are not just useful references, but objects of beauty. Maps, whether antiquarian or contemporary, have deep aesthetic appeal, they are artefacts whose colours, contours, hachures and even legends can be beguiling. As a traveller, I read maps not just for the information they reveal, but for the pleasure to be obtained from their beauty in the same way that as a writer I read the dictionary for the discovery of new words and the derivations of them.

At home today, in front of a computer screen, it's possible to click onto Google Earth's website and on it locate a satellite photograph of any continent, country, capital, suburb or street in the world, and zoom in on it with a clarity that enables the viewer to determine the condition of the pot-plants on the back deck. This technology has shrunk the entire Earth to computer screen size. Similarly, Global Positioning Systems mounted on a car's dashboard can verbally guide the driver through the maze of streets of a foreign city anywhere in the world.

But just as television has not replaced the book, personal GPS systems and satellite photographs have not yet replaced the printed map, a practical aid to travel which can be pored over and deciphered at a roadside lay-by, a town square café or in bed.

For almost as long as there have been travellers, there have been maps. The very earliest ones – carved on clay tablets in Babylon two and a half thousand years ago – showed Babylon and its surrounding towns, encircled by oceans. Unknown territories beyond the known world were the subject of speculation, much of it imaginatively depicted by way of broaching sea monsters and human heads expelling air from their mouths to represent winds.

The most significant early contribution to cartography was the map attributed to Claudius Ptolemy, a Greek mathematician and astronomer who lived in the second century AD. Ptolemy's map represents the known world of his age, including as it does the Mediterranean, North Africa, Western Europe and Scandinavia. The earliest road maps were drawn in the thirteenth century, in strip form, mainly for the benefit of merchants and pilgrims travelling through Europe. These overland maps include the most conspicuous man-made landmarks along the route, mainly castles and cathedrals, to help guide travellers to their destinations.

Meanwhile, on the other side of the world, Chinese explorers were making bold voyages from the land they called the 'Middle Kingdom' and thought of as the very centre of the world. They chartered much of South-East Asia, including the island nations known today as the Philippines and Indonesia, and some believe they also discovered the west coast of Australia. Chinese map-makers were also industrious, recording the voyages of their regional discoveries in meticulous detail.

From the fifteenth century onwards, European explorers and

navigators ventured beyond their home continent, heralding the Age of Exploration. Tentatively and courageously, they sailed as far as Southern Africa, the Far East and the Americas, confirming as they did so that early mathematicians were right – the Earth was a sphere. In 1520 Ferdinand Magellan's expedition entered, then crossed the Pacific Ocean. The remnants of the expedition eventually made it back to Spain in 1523, minus their leader, who had been killed in the Philippines in 1521. Just 18 of the 266 men who had set out three years earlier survived, but the Earth had at last been circumnavigated. Accompanying this era of exploration and discovery was a comparable expansion in map-making, as the new geographical knowledge was recorded.

For much of the sixteenth century, Rome and Venice led the European world in map production, but later the Low Countries – Holland and Belgium – came to dominate cartography. The most famous map-maker of this period was the Flemish Gerard Mercator, who also coined the word 'atlas'. Mercator is best known for his map projection, published in 1569. Now that the Earth had been confirmed as a sphere, a vexed problem for cartographers was how to accurately depict it on a map's flat surface. Globes could do this, but it was impractical to carry a globe around. The problem became greater with the need to navigate with a minimum of risk during prolonged ocean voyages, while at the same time taking into account the curvature of the Earth.

Mercator circumvented the flat/round problem by producing a map in which the distance between the lines of latitude increases away from the equator. This 'Mercator projection' global representation has endured, in spite of the fact that the size of the lands in high latitudes – such as Greenland in the Northern Hemisphere and Antarctica in the Southern Hemisphere – are distorted, being shown as much larger than they really are, while those in low latitudes, such as the Indian subcontinent, are too small. Since few travellers go to Greenland or Antarctica, their inflated size on a Mercator projection map is of little consequence, although the many people who go to India can be surprised to find that it takes much longer to get from Kerala in the south to Uttar Pradesh in the north than they had anticipated.

Like pieces of a giant jigsaw, continents, islands, sounds and promontories were gradually added to maps of the world during the voyages of discovery that took place in the seventeenth century. A growth in printing techniques during the same period culminated in a remarkably accurate map of the world being produced in Amsterdam in 1630. Employing Mercator's projection and with an effective use of colour, the map depicted a world three-quarters complete, lacking only North America above 60 degrees north latitude, the Arctic and Antarctica, and Australia and New Zealand. The equator and the Tropics of Cancer and Capricorn are included. This map is also a work of art, embellished with a frieze of landscapes and fantastic sea creatures.

However by halfway through the eighteenth century the islands of Oceania and the continents of Australia and Antarctica still remained unchartered. Dutchman Abel Tasman tentatively charted the west coast of New Zealand as far as the northern extremity of the North Island. European scholars and voyagers must have often stared at Tasman's incomplete map and wondered just what lay to the east of the mountainous coast the Dutchman had sketched. I too have stared at that work in progress, the unfinished symphony that is Tasman's chart of New Zealand, and wondered if Abel had yearned to come back and finish the job. Or had he been so terrified by his Maori welcome in Golden Bay, which he named Murderers' Bay, that he didn't care whether he returned or not … I suspect it was the latter.

Another 127 years were to pass before the answer to the question of what lay to the east of Tasman's map was provided. It had long been postulated by European scholars that there must be a 'Great Southern Continent', or '*Terra Australis Incognita*' in the Southern Hemisphere, to counter-balance the land mass of Eurasia and so maintain the stability of the planet. The discovery, charting and surveying of this Southern Continent became the aim of rival European nations, particularly Britain and France, during the second half of the eighteenth century.

It was the man who was probably the greatest navigator of them all, James Cook (1728-1779), who added the last major pieces to the Earth jigsaw. During his three long, arduous voyages during the second half of the eighteenth century, Cook was an assiduous charter of the coastlines he explored. In doing so he also proved the non-existence of *Terra Australis Incognita*. Cook's charts were published upon his return to England, and like his journals, attracted enormous interest. His chart of New Zealand (published in 1772) is one of the finest ever made, depicting the coastlines of the North and South Islands with remarkable accuracy. However, lacking a means of establishing longitude accurately while at sea resulted in Cook underestimating the width of both islands, so that they appear rather anorexic on his 1772 'Chart of New Zealand'.

The longitudinal value of a position on Earth was the distance reflected by the difference between local time and the time at an established location. Fifteen degrees of longitude was equivalent to a time difference of one hour. Everything was in the timing, but in Cook's era there was no accurate and reliable timepiece that could be used at sea.

It was not until Englishman John Harrison (1693-1776) perfected a marine chronometer that it became possible to accurately determine longitude at sea. Once Harrison's timepiece came into use it only required the establishment of a standard position – called zero longitude, or the prime meridian – before longitude could be measured accurately. In 1884 a single prime meridian was established at Greenwich, London, and universally accepted. (One of my more exciting journeys was the one which took me to Greenwich and allowed me to bestride the bronze marker in the ground there which demarcates the Prime Meridian, thus allowing me to have one foot in the

Western Hemisphere and the other in the Eastern. Although this can be done anywhere along the line of zero degrees longitude, from Ghana to Greenland, there was something special about straddling the Prime Meridian in Greenwich, the place where it was designated.)

With the advent of manned flight, aerial photography and satellite imagery, cartography has been extended to include formerly inaccessible parts of the Earth, so that no part of it remains unscrutinised and unmapped. Sophisticated computer technology has led to digital imagery that further enhances map production. Continents can be shown in three dimensions, their sierras leaping from the page; ocean floors, submarine mountain chains and chasms are laid bare, capes, bays and estuaries are depicted in all their myriad configurations. Today's maps can show the entire world, the moon, Mars, or the streets comprising a city block. Digital maps are widely available on the Internet.

But for the traveller, and particularly the car driver in a strange land, it is the hand-held, large-scale map which is still the most practical travel companion and guide.

The best map I ever owned was one of England's south-east region. New to Britain and living in Reigate, Surrey, an hour's drive south of London, I quickly found this map to be an essential reference. It covered the lower right-hand corner of England, with the great spreading node of London near the top of the map, its motorways, A, B and C roads (I quickly learned to use those terms) radiating out from the metropolis. The map showed public footpaths too, criss-crossing the countryside. The south coast was depicted in detail, along with the Vale of Kent, the North Downs, South Downs and the Weald in between. The marshes of Dickens' coast, east of London, were included, while dotted lines extending outwards from Dover and Dieppe marked ferry routes across the Channel.

I planned all my weekend sojourns with that map, selecting routes away from the A23 and the A25, revelling in the fact that now I could choose an almost infinite number of alternative routes through the South-East, ducking and diving and choosing roads through villages and towns with names such as Nether Upping, Greater Snoring, Mugswell, Lower Piddle and Dorking. Even on my drive to work in the small Surrey town of Horley there were a number of possible rural by-ways that allowed me to avoid the busy A23. I settled on using the B5003, a narrow country lane that plunged down the face of the North Downs, then wound across a lowland of pastures and oak trees, crossed a meandering river called the Mole via an ancient stone bridge, and passed a shingled pub called The Wheatsheaf before reaching the outskirts of the place where I worked. What a delightful contrast to driving in New Zealand, I thought, where there was usually only one way to go, and if there was an alternative road only a tractor could cope with it.

All of England – all of Britain – was covered by such 'Inch-to-the-Mile' series maps, and they guided me back and forth and up and down England for several years.

Once I went to France – to the Languedoc region, in the south-west – and neglected to take a regional map with me. I had a hired car and was staying in a village called Pouzolles, a place too small to be registered on anything but the most detailed of maps. All I had with me was a Michelin map showing the whole of France. Over the course of the week, there was not one day when I didn't get lost. I wasted hours trying to find a suitable route back to Pouzolles, and by the time I did so I had become very ill-tempered indeed. Navigating largely by guesswork, in a country where I had to drive on the right, resulted in wrong turnings, missings of by-passes, and blunderings into the centre of crowded towns where the streets were invariably one-way. Every day in this state of 'perdu' I would inevitably come across 'chausee deformé' (road works) and 'detournement' (diversion) signs, which further complicated my journey back to the village, all adding to my stress levels.

Towards the end of my stay I visited a New Zealand man, Barry Devereux, who lived with his English artist wife Jacqueline, just outside Pouzolles. After I recounted my navigational problems to them, Barry produced a regional Michelin map of the Languedoc region. 'Here, borrow this,' he said, handing it over.

I did, and the Languedoc fell immediately into place. Every road and every village – even Pouzolles – appeared on it. Everything from autoroutes (in bold yellow and red stripes) to scenic back-roads (outlined in green) was included on the map, allowing me to negotiate my way happily to tiny but divinely formed Languedoc destinations such as St Guilhelm-le-Desert, Minervois and St Gervais. It was like another Age of Discovery. I had learned a crucial travel lesson: always, *always* buy the most detailed map available of the area you'll be visiting, and keep it with you at all times.

Of all maps used by travellers, perhaps the most often used is not strictly a map at all. This is the plan of the London Underground. Produced by London Regional Transport, it is a stylised representation of the thirteen train line systems that convey people across London from north to south and west to east. Nothing is more emblematic of the metropolis of London than this map; it is reproduced on posters, postcards, tea towels and even the mouse pad beside the computer on which I am writing this chapter.

There is only one problem with the London Underground Map: it is not drawn to scale. This can create unforseen difficulties for non-Londoners trying to negotiate their way around the city.

Once, while staying at Willesden Green in NW London, I had

to get to the post office in Harlesden, where a registered package was being held for me. The London Underground map showed that it was a long way from Willesden Green to Harlesden, but that there was a station there. So I took the Underground from Willesden Green south to Baker Street, on the Jubilee Line, and changed there to the Bakerloo Line, bound for Harlesden.

Disembarking at the Harlesden station, I set off for the local post office. As I did so it began to rain. I had no coat. I sheltered under trees, walked on, then sheltered again. The rain grew stronger, running down my neck and eventually pooling uncomfortably in the bottom of my shoes. I trudged on, past un-verandahed shops which provided no shelter, sloshing through puddles and stepping around sleeping vagrants, until after an hour and a half, and totally sodden, I reached the Harlesden post office. There I uplifted my package – a Eurorail ticket from London to Paris – and set off on my return journey to the Harlesden station. Bear in mind it was January and therefore very cold as well as wet, and somewhere just off the High Street – surely one of the most dispiriting places in London – I took a wrong turn. I mooched on, peering through the grey rain for the Underground station which would eventually get me back to where I was staying. Then I looked up at the shops I was approaching. They looked familiar. They *were* familiar. It was Willesden Green High Street, the same street which, in spite of being shown on the Underground map as a vast distance from Harlesden, was in fact barely one kilometre away. I could have walked from one to the other in ten minutes.

So for all its multi-coloured geometry and attractively interlacing lines, I have never since quite trusted the London Underground map.

This resentment had not been assuaged some time later when I next sought the help of the Underground. This time I wanted to get from Chiswick, in SW London, to Richmond, on the other side of the Thames. As it was a Sunday afternoon and not raining, I decided to walk along the river from Chiswick to my destination. Kew Bridge, I knew, crossed the Thames not far north of Chiswick and led directly to Kew Gardens, then Richmond. As the route looked straightforward, I didn't bother to take my *London A-Z* map book with me.

However, after an hour of walking, I discovered that the distance to Kew Bridge was in fact much greater than I had expected. Moreover, I found that in order to get to the bridge I had to walk alongside the A4, a 'dual carriageway' along which every boy racer and grown-up racer in England was hurtling towards the West. I couldn't even see the Thames, although I knew it must be on the other side of the A4. To walk across this de facto motorway seemed impossible, so I walked on, without a map or any landmarks to guide me. What seemed like hours passed. This was no Sunday stroll; it was turning into a route march. Bugger this, I decided, instead of walking I would take the tube to Richmond. Pulling the Underground map from my pocket, I saw that it showed the District Line running directly south from a station called Chiswick Park to Kew Gardens, before terminating in Richmond. Simple. Now all I had to do was find Chiswick Park Station.

But I couldn't. After another half hour of walking, I was almost totally disorientated. Eventually I came to a street that seemed to be heading north, and roughly towards the station I sought. I turned into the street. It was long and lined on both sides by large Tudor-style semi-detached houses. Plane trees in early summer leaf grew from the berms and the houses' small front gardens were bright with roses and pansies. The street was also lined with shiny late model Rovers, BMWs, Audis and Land Rovers. I had obviously stumbled into a neighbourhood described in England as 'upper-middle-class', one of hundreds of such districts that are common in SW London, and one where directions to Chiswick Park Underground Station would be simple to find.

Seeing a middle-aged couple about to get into a gleaming

green Jaguar parked outside one of the houses, I approached them.

'Excuse me, I'm a visitor here. I'm trying to get to Richmond by train. Can you tell me where I can catch one?'

The reactions on the faces of both the man and the woman told me immediately that I had made a serious mistake. The man – tall, balding and dressed in checked jacket and roll neck jumper – blinked in confusion. His wife, blonde and plump-faced, wearing a camelhair coat, bore an expression of alarm. I realised why. These were people who had probably never been on public transport in their entire lives. The man stretched his neck, peered about distractedly, then stammered, 'I should try British Rail.' He pointed in the direction of the A4.

'It's Sunday,' I pointed out. 'I don't think British Rail trains will be running today.'

The woman looked at me darkly, as if I had exposed myself. Then she frowned and said, 'What about the Underground?'

Her husband nodded decisively, and with a note of triumph in his voice said, 'Yes, yes, the Underground! I should take the Underground.'

'I was going to,' I replied, 'but I can't find the station.' I looked from the man to the woman. 'Where is Chiswick Park Station from here?'

Panic struck the man. His head swung about like a weathervane in a gale before his eyes alighted on his wife. Avoiding his gaze, she stared at the ground. *Christ, neither of them knows where it is*, I realised. Then, inhaling very slowly, the man took his hands from his pockets and placed them behind his back. He looked up and down the street, wincing, as if he was in pain. Which in a way he must have been, unwilling to admit to a stranger from a far-off land that he didn't know his own railway system. His wife was still staring at the berm, her face in a state of crumpled embarrassment. But the man was having none of that. Drawing himself up to his full height, he pointed north, up the street.

'I should walk in that direction,' he said crisply, and with total authority. 'At the end of this street you will come to the dual carriageway.' He paused, then drew breath again. 'I should cross the dual carriageway. With care, of course. And then … and then … I should …' his expression became wild once more. '… I should … *ask again!*'

Such are the perils of finding oneself about in London. Asking a local almost always proved fruitless, and relying on the Underground Map as an aid to navigation should be done with caution.

A good map, though, remains indispensable, wherever you are.

New Zealand maps, once prosaic, are now as good as you can get anywhere. The 1:50 000 topographic series is lovely to look at, as well as being extremely useful. When I was researching my historical novel, *Alice & Luigi*, much of which is set on the Makara coast, the Wellington 1:50 000 R27, R28 map was my constant reference. Far more than photographs – although I used them too – the map gave me a real feeling for the landscape that my characters inhabited. It gave me hill heights and bay names and landmark titles, and its subtle shading and contours allowed the district's uplands to spring out at me. When the characters in my novel moved up to the Kapiti coast, I obtained the neighbouring map, R26, and drew heavily on that too. Its graphic representation of Kapiti Island enabled me to construct with some confidence the scenes in the novel which are set on and around the island, without my ever having put a foot upon it.

I now also have a new 1:1000 000 map of New Zealand, which is not only a model of geographic clarity it can also be referred to in a kayak, on a white-water raft or a jet-boat, because it's completely waterproof.

# The English Traveller

Years of looking at maps of England had instilled in me a desire to see where the River Thames began. On these maps the Thames wriggles and loops its way across England, then meanders through London before flowing into the North Sea. Most maps show it starting as a mere squiggle in Gloucestershire, but I wanted to find out about the source of that squiggle. Did it emerge as a trickling spring or burst forth from the hillside? For how long did the squiggle go before it grew into a proper river? I had to find out.

At 215 miles (346km) long, the Thames is a mere dribble compared to the Danube (2291 miles/3688km) or the Volga (1770 miles/2850km). Even the Seine is more than twice the length of the Thames. But no other water course is so saturated in history. By the time the waters of the Thames reach the western outskirts of London they have already flowed past some of England's most venerable landmarks, including Oxford University, Runnymede, Windsor Castle and Hampton Court. From Oxford downstream the Thames is a considerable river and a vital artery. All along its lower reaches it has been tamed and modified, used as a pleasure boat playground, a source of reservoir water and – from London to the sea – a shipping highway. The London stretch of the Thames is featured everywhere, especially on postcards and travel brochures, so it is virtually synonymous with the city it crosses from west to east. But what is the river like upstream from Oxford?

England's wonderful Ordnance Survey maps provided an essential reference in the planning of my Thames source-seeking expedition. They showed me every footpath, towpath, tributary, lock, lane and pub along the river. The maps also showed that thanks to the marvellous Thames Path, it's possible to walk alongside the river for almost its entire length. This trail allows visitors to leave their cars and stroll along the river on selected sections, to savour the rural birdlife, wildflowers, riverside pubs and villages. Upstream from Oxford, the Thames meanders towards the West Country, passing villages such as Shifford, Duxford, Radcot and Buscot. Here the river forms the border between the counties of Oxfordshire to the north and Berkshire on its south side.

Studying the map, I see that I'm still some way from my goal, the source. Feeling like the fearless Victorian explorer Sir Richard Burton in search of the source of the Nile, I drive west, taking roads as close to the Thames as possible, crossing a broad basin into which the river has incised itself. On the southern side are meadows and woodlands, crop-fields and ancient stone farmhouses, on the north bank lanes wind around dozens of lakes and reservoirs. The Thames here is still broad – about 20 metres across – and slow-flowing, its sedgy edges and low banks blending with willows, hawthorn, chestnut and oak trees. It's early summer, and the land is lush and leafy, brimming with fresh growth. Beyond the banks are juicy pastures, grazing dairy herds and fields of young 'corn' (i.e. wheat) and golden-flowered rapeseed. The square towers of medieval village churches stand out among the pale green of the spreading oaks and chestnuts; sylvan scenes which could have come straight from a Constable painting.

First stop is the hamlet of Radcot. Here the river splits in two briefly and the Thames Path crosses from the south bank to the north. One of the two bridges at Radcot was built by the Romans, and is the oldest of all the Thames' bridges. Humpbacked and one-way, it sprouts traffic lights at both ends, an incongruous sight. When the light turns green, I drive across the bridge, keeping a watchful eye for chariots coming the other way.

About eight kilometres upriver from Radcot, and backing onto the Thames, is Kelmscott Manor, a fifteenth-century manor house which was home to the noted poet, designer and socialist, William Morris (1834-1896). He founded the Kelmscott Press here in 1890, and for a time shared the manor with the pre-Raphaelite painter and poet Dante Gabriel Rossetti. However an over-familiarity with Morris's beautiful wife, Jane, whom Rossetti used as a model, led to an estrangement between the two men.

Kelmscott Manor contains many examples of Morris's superb fabric designs, and the gardens around the house are delightful. A tiny tributary of the Thames passes alongside the manor's outbuildings.

On the way from Kelmscott to the next village on the river, Buscot, I also pass from Oxfordshire into Gloucestershire. At Buscot is the first lock on the Thames, St Johns, and the Old Parsonage, an early eighteenth-century house of pale yellow stone. A wharf at Buscot is a reminder that the Thames is still navigable to this stage. Locally made brandy was once sent from here downriver to France for distillation, I read to my surprise. Brandy *to* France *from* England? That's like exporting Yorkshire pudding from Paris to London. Beside St Johns lock is a pretty lock-keeper's cottage, a dizzying weir and a sculpture of a reclining Father Thames, originally made for the 1851 Great Exhibition in London.

Lechlade, just a meander away from Buscot, is a very agreeable market town which marks the upper limit of the navigable Thames. A canal, now disused, once linked the Thames with the Severn River and made Lechlade one of the busiest inland ports in England. Here are many antique shops and one of the best-known Thameside pubs, The Trout. The river at Lechlade is home for a long pod of narrow houseboats tidily tucked up against the riverbank or moored inside a small marina.

Just up from Lechlade the 'teenage' Thames is joined by one of its larger tributaries, the Coln, at a junction overhung by willows and guarded by a seventeenth-century millhouse. The Thames here is sluggish, its bronze-coloured waters disturbed only by gliding swans and ducks.

Now the Thames, flowing directly from the west, becomes the frontier between Gloucestershire and Wiltshire, but is navigable only by very small launches. About fourteen kilometres further upriver from Lechlade is Cricklade, a pretty little town built on a Roman road and dating back to Anglo-Saxon times. Above Cricklade there is no statutory right of navigation on the Thames. Understandably so, for now the river is considerably narrower.

Standing on the bridge on Cricklade's High Street, I can see that here the river is only about five metres wide. But it's swift-flowing, deep and perfectly clear, its bed trailing long green weeds which wave about like streamers in the brisk current, bringing to mind the river in Tennyson's The Lady of Shalott. 'Tirra lirra' by the river, indeed. There's something hypnotically beautiful about the river at this, its juvenile stage, probably because the river-watcher knows where the current will eventually flow. This same water that I'm staring into will later flow past the Houses of Parliament, the Tower of London, under Tower Bridge and past Greenwich, on its journey to the North Sea.

Upstream from Cricklade the Thames' banks are thick with brambles, hawthorn, Queen Anne's Lace and beds of nettles which sting me as I brush past them while tramping along an overgrown path. Now I really feel like Sir Richard Burton, suffering to find my river's source. Studying the Ordnance Map very closely, I note that it shows the Thames swinging back into Gloucestershire, then flowing through the straggling village of Ashton Keynes. But back on the road, I see that the river is now much more vaguely defined. The surrounding land is so low-lying it's marshy, the river has broadened again and the bed of the river itself is so weedy it's almost part of the marsh. As the lane swings away from the river, and as there's no time to walk the Thames Path before darkness falls, I decide to try and reach the source by road.

Easier said than done. Most roads in this part of England lead to Cirencester, a Roman town and the largest one in the area, but on my map the Thames' source appears to be a few miles west of the town. Skirting around Cirencester, I drive in the general direction of the putative source, Thames Head. On either side of a busy road there are meadows. Glancing left and right through the hedgerows that line the road, I can see no sign whatsoever of a river, just buttercup-studded fields. Then, halfway along a stretch of the road, I see a sign pointing right: Source of the Thames. Another sign also points right declaring Thames Head. *This is it!*

Leaving the car in a layby, I climb a stile into the meadow. But there's no watercourse here, no spring magically bubbling up out of the meadow from a cleft in a rock as I imagined there would be. There's a sign pointing towards a low hill, though, and a footpath that crosses a muddy field where black and white cows become skittish at my approach. A little further on, maybe a kilometre or so, there's a small depression in the ground, filled with flat stones. A nearby notice proclaims it to be the 'Source of the Thames'.

But it's an oxymoron as well as an anti-climax; the source of the Thames is dry. Supposedly, beneath the stones is a spring; and right now it's not springing, despite the fact that this is indeed the official source of the river. The Romans, the notice adds, called the river the Isis.

Later, studying yet another map of the river's course, I read a revealing footnote: 'The source of the Thames is disputed'. Apparently there are several rivulets draining down from the Cotswold Hills, and one had to be chosen as the official source. Someone picked the pile of flat stones and the subterranean spring, then declared the district Thames Head. There the Thames conservators first placed that sculpture of Old Father Thames, after the 1851 Great Exhibition. But when the source of the great river became contentious, a compromise was reached and Old Father Thames was moved to St Johns Lock at Buscot, where the Thames is indisputably the Thames.

In every respect, the Thames and its source is a very English story.

The base for carrying out my intrepid journey to the Thames' source is a village in Berkshire which, for reasons that should become clear, I will call Willingham. The village has one wide main street. Its core consists of stone buildings, three antique pubs and a fourteenth-century church surrounded by gravestones which have settled into crazy angles. In the High Street, along with the pubs, are, respectively, a newsagent, an off-licence, a haberdashery, a ferociously expensive restaurant, a small supermarket and an Indian curry house. Lanes run off the High Street to a housing estate on one side and meadows on the other. There are footpaths through the fields through which I sometimes used to walk to neighbouring villages, and stone bridges that cross the Bristol to London line, along which high-speed trains hurtle several times a day.

From the meadows outside the village there are views south to the long, undulating green wall that constitutes the Berkshire Downs. Following the crest of the Downs was an ancient walkway, the Ridgeway, sections of which I walked on several occasions. On a clear day the path provides wonderful views of the western counties of England. A particular feature along the Ridgeway is the Vale of the White Horse, above which is the White Horse of Uffington, an abstract image of a horse carved into the turf of the downs' escarpment. This image resembles a horse Picasso might have sketched, but it's been there since the Bronze Age. The White Horse of Uffington is the oldest and most beautiful of England's chalk hill figures, its impressionistic white lines dramatically visible against the green turf of the surrounding escarpment.

The White Horse drew me back time after time, its antiquity and mystery a magnetic force. Legend has it that this is also the very place where Saint George slew the dragon, and where the dragon's blood flowed out onto the ground; grass has never grown here since. Spoiling this story somewhat is the fact that every year the outline of the white horse and the dragon's bleeding are scoured by volunteers (done in order to keep the tracery clear and chalk-white), a procedure that has been followed for almost 100 generations.

As with Stonehenge, 50 kilometres to the south, the Ridgeway's prehistoric sites have become in recent years the focus for neo-pagan rites, particularly during the summer solstice. Twenty minutes' walk west of the White Horse is Waylands Smithy, a 5000-year-old burial chamber built over an even older 'barrow' or burial mound. According to local legend, any horse left here overnight would be shod by Wayland, the Anglo-Saxon blacksmith god. Waylands Smithy and the White Horse attract dozens of visitors every year on 21 June, or so says a local in a nearby pub . Cars parked in the vicinity, he claims, were all rented vehicles, so those that drove up there for solstice sport could not be identified. This suggests that what went on up there was something more than Morris Dancing, but when I press him for details he becomes flushed and evasive, indicating that he may have been more familiar with the solstice rites that he is prepared to admit.

Willingham, below the Vale of the White Horse, has the appearance of being little different to innumerable other villages in the west of England. But grafted onto the village is an academy that apparently trains people in the arts of military science. I was told about the establishment one night while enjoying some local hospitality in one of Willingham's pubs. Servicemen and women from all over the British Commonwealth come to study here, the proprietor of the Rat and Parrot tells me. To study what? I ask him. Mine host shrugs, then laughs. 'Ow ter find weapons of mass destruction, maybe?'

Surrounded by a high stone wall topped with razor wire, the academy can only be glimpsed as I drive past it. I can see that the grounds are extensive, but stands of trees conceal the interior. The longer I stay in the village, the more my curiosity is aroused. What exactly goes on in there? Who are the people being trained? What does the training consist of? But there is no way I can find out. Everything is top secret. The main entranceway, on the outskirts of Willingham, is heavily guarded by the British Army and bristles with suspicion and security. I watch every vehicle entering the establishment being searched, see the soldiers putting mirrors on long poles under them, sweeping their underbellies to see if bombs might be attached there. Everyone's passes are examined, their photos and other identity details scrutinised. After the London bombings, the British military authorities are taking no chances.

Then one afternoon, returning from a walk through the fields to the neighbouring village of Piddledown, I find myself alongside a section of the high wire-topped wall. And there, set into the wall, I notice a narrow wooden gate. Looking at it more closely, I see that it is locked, and that there is a key pad set into the gate. As I peer at the pad, an elderly woman comes along. Pale-faced, with sagging cheeks, she is wearing a headscarf and grey overcoat, and is carrying a supermarket bag. 'Hello, love,' she says cheerily. Then, putting the bag down with obvious relief, she stops to chat. She asks me where I am from, and volunteers that fact that she is a widow who's lived in Willingham for 47 years. Pointing to the gate, I say, 'What's this for?'

'To get into the academy,' she tells me.

'But who uses it?' I ask.

'The village people, if they need to.'

'But it's locked. And it's got a key code,' I point out.

'Yes, but the village people know the code,' the woman replies. 'The army changes the code once a month, but everyone finds out what it is.' Peering up at me, she asks, 'Do you want to go in?'

'Yes.'

'Well, this month the code's ...' Her brow creases with concentration. '765 ...98. Yes, that's right, it's 76598 just now.'

She brushes past me, pokes the numbers with a knobbly forefinger, then pushes. The gate swings open. 'There you go,' she says matter-of-factly. 'Don't forget; 76598.'

Thanking her, I stroll through the gate, close it after me and commit the five digits to memory.

There is a concrete pathway following the inside perimeter of the wall. I follow it, through a copse of oak and ash trees, bright green with their early summer foliage. There is no other soul in sight. After a time the path emerges at an estate of neat, modern, semi-detached houses, laid out around several cul-de-sacs. I walk down the street. Still I come across no other people, but by one of the streets is a triangular sign on which is the symbol for a kangaroo, and under it the words, 'Next 2000km'. The housing here is for visiting Australian military personnel, I deduce. Good Ocker joke.

I walk on. The street ends at another grove of trees, but there is a pathway that I follow through the grove. It descends, then emerges at a lake, over which is a humped stone bridge. Water lily pads float on the lake, and several white swans and families of ducks come gliding towards me hopefully. The scene is bucolic. However my attention is taken not by the lake and the birds so much as the building atop the rise on the other side of the water. It's massive, a three-storeyed manor house, built of honey-coloured stone, with a crenellated roofline and many mullioned windows. Its provenance looks to me to be of the seventeenth or eighteenth century. Flower beds surround the building, giving way to a smooth, well-tended lawn which slopes down to the lake. I cross the bridge and walk up the slope to the imposing building.

The main entranceway is on the far side. A broad driveway leads up to the entrance, which is covered by a portico, over which the Union Jack flies. Further down the drive is a number of one-storeyed, modern buildings. I spot men and women in army, navy and air force uniforms, most carrying briefcases, walking briskly along the drive in both directions. I hesitate now, knowing I have no right whatsoever to be here. I have certainly already transgressed the anti-terrorism laws. I should just retrace my steps and return to the village via the little side entrance. But as I stare up at the lovely old building, I know I won't, because I yearn to see what it is like inside a top-secret military establishment. Fortunately I am dressed in respectable clothes for my ramble: corduroy trousers, turtle-neck jumper and sports jacket. And I had received a very short haircut from the village barber just a couple of days ago.

I walk over to the entrance, then up the steps and into the building.

Here is an anteroom, carpeted, with wainscotted walls and a large oak desk at one end. Eight-paned double doors with polished brass fittings separate the anteroom from the rest of the building. Behind the desk, a young woman in army greens sits staring at a computer screen. She takes not the slightest notice of me. I pull one of the double doors open and step inside the body of the building. There, I stop and stare.

The huge, carpeted room is filled with row upon row of bookshelves. The shelves are of dark wood, and the books they hold are all hardbacks. The room's ceiling is of white plaster, moulded into ornate patterns, and about 20 metres high. An enormous chandelier hangs from a large rose in the centre of the ceiling. A gallery runs around three sides of the upper part of the room, giving access to even more bookshelves, and a wide staircase with a polished wooden hand-rail leads up to the right, to what I presume are the upper floors of the building. Oil portraits of stern men in military uniform hang from the walls below the gallery. I am in the centre of a vast and venerable library. There is an atmosphere of peace and quietude in the place, of studiousness and serenity, like there used to be in libraries before the children took over.

A wide aisle goes down the centre of the room, with the rows of bookshelves running off to the left and right. I walk down the aisle, wondering at the scale and dignity of the huge room. It could well have been the manor house's original ballroom, I guess. Turning down one of the bookshelf aisles, I look at the spines of the books. History, Art History, Military History, Political Science, Classics. The place would be perfect for a research student. But exactly what kind of research goes on here?

At the far end of the room I come to a clear area where there are about a dozen carrels, each of which houses a computer. In a line along a wall to the right are several photocopiers. Some of the carrels are occupied by uniformed men and women, each frowning with concentration as they tap at their keyboards. Walking past them, I climb the wide, curving staircase. Halfway up is a landing, over which hangs a huge oil portrait of a bewigged, frock-coated man: The First Earl of Willingham (1636–1693), according to the plaque beneath. The staircase emerges at another floor, which is also filled with rows of bookshelves, these ones holding science books: botany, zoology, chemistry, physics. What a treasure house of resources and references! Walking back down the staircase, I pause on the landing to look down over the main room and its elegant gallery, its orderly ranks of bookshelves and the work space where the computers are. A thought occurrs to me and I rebuke myself. No, I couldn't possibly. I think again. But I could try. I'd come this far, after all.

The young woman working on the computer is in army uniform. She has two pips on each shoulder.

'Excuse me, Lieutenant, but is this computer being used?'

She looks up and smiles obligingly. 'No Sir, no one's using that one.' She is in her early 30s, with bobbed blonde hair. Her accent is northern English.

'Thank you.'

I sit down at the carrel next to hers and click the mouse. The mouse pad, I notice, carries a picture of a tank in attack mode. The computer's screen comes into view, showing Windows XP and various icons. Needing the Internet, I click on it. A box flashes up, asking me for my password. Of course, I have to have a password. As I click my tongue with exasperation, the Lieutenant hears me. She leans over.

'Do you have a problem, Sir?'

'Yes, I'm …I'm trying to get access to the Internet – for my email – and it won't let me.'

'Oh. Let me see if I can help, Sir.'

I surrender my seat to her, and she sits and stares at the screen. Then, turning, she asks, 'You have to enter your password. What is it?'

Caught. Exposed. Sprung. I think as fast as I can. 'Well,

actually, I haven't got one yet. I've just arrived here. From New Zealand.'

Her face lights up. 'Oh, really? How long are you here for?'

'Just a few days. And I really need to catch up on my email.' I sigh. 'But I haven't got a password yet.' Recalling an age-old army gripe, I add, 'They're taking so long.'

Everyone who'd been anywhere near the military (and I'd been a National Serviceman in the 1960s) knew who *they* are.

She rolls her eyes in sympathy, then runs her tongue around her neat mouth. She has a very light application of pale lipstick, I notice, and a beautifully clear English complexion. 'I know,' she says, 'it takes ages to go through Admin.' She thinks for a moment. 'Look, I'll let you have some of my tabs.' She goes back to her desk and fiddles in a briefcase. Tabs?

Handing me several small slips of blue paper, each about three inches long, she says, 'There you are, Sir, here're six tabs. You just click on Login, then key in the numbers and letters on the tab. Each one gives you fifteen minutes of the Internet. Will that keep you going until they get you your password?'

I stare at the pieces of paper. Each one has a row of eight mixed upper-case letters and numbers on it. 'Oh, yes. Yes, that'll be quite enough. Thank you very much, Lieutenant.'

My pretty friend smiles. 'Good luck, Sir. I hope you enjoy your time with us.' As she takes the seat at her own computer again, she asks, 'What part of New Zealand are you from?'

'Auckland. Devonport.'

'Aaah, Devonport,' she said, knowingly. 'I knew you were a navy man.'

And so for the rest of my time in Willingham I have the full use of the academy library facilities. Always entering by the side gate and never once challenged, neither in the grounds or at the academy's entrance, I use the library's computers to email friends, contact publishers, photocopy maps from the library's atlases, plan touring routes in Oxfordshire and read up about the history of the manor house. (Completed in 1679 by the First Earl of Willingham, lived in by his heirs and successors until 1940, when it was requisitioned from the Eighth Earl of Willingham under the wartime emergency regulations proclaimed by the British Government and in that year converted to a centre for military intelligence.) Everyone greets me in a genial way, whether they pass me walking through the woods surrounding the manor, see me feeding bread to the ducks and swans on the lake or come upon me browsing among the bookshelves.

And ever since then, every time I see a news report of the British Military at work in Kosovo, Iraq or Afghanistan, I feel a little surge of sympathy for those brave women and men.

# The Flying Traveller

In the late 1960s plane travel overtook sea travel as the commonest method of getting from one continent to another. The commercial advent of the so-called 'Jumbo Jet', the Boeing 747 in 1970, was the aviation breakthrough the travel businesses had been waiting for. Now several hundred people at a time could be moved quickly and relatively easily around the world.

They have been moving ever since. Once the mode of travel of the rich, travel by air is now the domain of the masses, in economy class, the huddled masses. In 1951 the return airfare from Auckland to Sydney on a Solent flying boat was nearly 51 pounds (over 100 dollars). Now, 50 years later, when incomes have increased a hundred-fold, it's possible to get an airfare on the same route for only four times the 1951 price. To fly to London from Auckland one way in 1951 cost 279 pounds, a whole year's average income. In other words, over half a century ago, it cost the equivalent of tens of thousands of today's dollars to fly right around the world. Today you can do it for less than 2000 dollars, which many people earn in a fortnight. It may not be as comfortable to fly now as it was in the days of the silver service Solents, but it is miles cheaper. Along with the long-established carriers, budget airlines have sprung up all over the world, providing ultra-cheap flights to the most popular destinations.

Flying is not only cheap and commonplace, it is also amazingly safe, at least in the western world. When one considers just how many planes are taking off from and landing at hectically busy airports (typically, one every two minutes) and flying along congested air corridors, the safety of flying is remarkable. For example, in the US in 2005 there were 10,935,000 scheduled passenger departures by air, and there were only 0.027 fatal accidents per 100,000 departures. It's said that more people die from bee stings in the US than from air crashes, although in the republics which comprise the former Soviet Union, the bees are almost certainly beaten into second place by the planes. Generally, however, what is potentially the most perilous form of travel is anything but. A passenger plane crash with loss of life is sufficiently unusual to make headlines all over the world.

Like most other travellers, I've flown frequently. I have flown right across Siberia, around the edge of Antarctica, across the Himalayas, over the vastness of the Pacific Ocean and close to the North Pole, and I've never felt unsafe while doing so. There's been some occasional turbulence, but nothing that a tightened seat belt couldn't fix. I was totally unafraid of flying.

Then one day I flew from Auckland to Christchurch.

It was a November morning, and conditions were fine as the Air New Zealand 737 took off from Auckland. We curved down the coast of the North Island. Conditions were still clear. As the plane banked to follow its route across the north of the South Island, Farewell Spit appeared, like a sickle poised to reap the waters of Cook Strait

Suddenly, with no warning whatsoever, the plane plummeted for several seconds. Straight down. It was as if the bottom had dropped out of the world. A collective gasp went through the cabin. Then, just as suddenly, the plane shot upwards. The warning lights flashed on, we all scrambled for our seat belts, coupling clicks were heard everywhere. 'Cabin crew, take your seats please,' came an announcement from the flight deck. The flight attendants scurried down the heaving aisle. Seconds later, we were all hurled downward again. A couple of cries came from the passengers. Gripping my arm rests, I tried not to think about what might be happening outside. I thought the turbulence would quickly subside, as it usually did.

It didn't. The bad air continued, tossing the plane this way, then the other, in a series of yawing, giddying movements. I felt the skin on my neck turning greasy. The plane was like a twig, tossed about by a river in spate. Up, down, sideways, all with sickening suddenness. In front of me, heads were pushed back against the seats' headrests. All the way down the plane I could see the tops of the other passengers' heads, moving from side to side in perfect unison with the plane's lurching, like some crazily choreographed chorus line. Side to side, up and down, side to side, up and down. The young man next to me had gone rigid, his fingers gripping the arms of the seat like talons. We were all aware of the mountains, rock, ice and snow below us.

The convulsions went on. That there were no announcements from the flight deck I thought an ominous sign. When I glanced to my right, past my frozen neighbour and out the window, I saw that the plane's wing was flapping up and down madly. It seemed impossible that mere alloy could withstand that furious battering for much longer. Turning away from the horrifying sight, I heard sobbing from across the aisle. It was coming from the youngish, be-suited businessman who had checked in self-importantly just ahead of me. The plane was not so much flying now as jerking off, each spasm seeming to bring it closer and closer to its climax, each spasm matched by a wave of nausea which passed through me, then returned with the plane's next lurch. Pushing my head back as hard as I could, I closed my eyes and pulled a map of the South Island down onto the monitor in my mind. The Alps must end soon, then we would be over the Canterbury Plains. No more mountains, no more turbulence.

Wrong. The plains appeared, the clouds dissolved, but the hurtling and jerking continued. Clear air turbulence now. The worst kind, evidently. The plane dropped, rose, rocked, dropped again, constantly. Still there was no word from the flight deck. But realistically, what could they say? 'Ah, ladies and gentlemen, as you can tell, we are experiencing a little turbulence. This will only be momentary.' Oh, sure. I imagined the pilot and co-pilot concentrating entirely on the ground below, searching for an area of clear land on which to try and put the plane down safely. We were, I now knew, all going to go down together. Glancing to my right, I saw a neat patchwork of cropland and pine plantations. That was where we would go down, that was where we were going to live or die. Perhaps live if we missed the trees, certainly die if we hit them. I didn't want to die in the South Island. I didn't want to die. Dimly I was aware that the descent had begun, but there was no comfort in this knowledge because the plane still seemed totally under the control of the elements. It plummeted again, tipped wildly from side to side, then swept up again. Many of the passengers were sobbing uncontrollably now. The young man next to me was making little whimpering noises, like a wounded dog, and his knuckles had gone pure white. The plane dropped yet again, and seconds later, shot up once more. Glancing in terror to my right, I saw the outskirts of Christchurch coming into view. Yet even over the city, the buffeting and tossing continued. Why, why? Then, several endless minutes later, the runway rushed up to meet us. My stomach was stuck in my throat, and I only just stopped myself from vomiting. The most terrifying flight of my life was over.

As we disembarked, no one spoke. The faces of the flight attendants were like tallow, their eyes glazed. Several passengers – not all of them women – were still tearful. But we had survived. Was it the notorious Canterbury Nor'wester that had caused the extreme turbulence? Certainly it was the right time of year, and outside the terminal, the strong dessicating wind tore at my hair. And from that day on, I have always approached a flight into Christchurch with trepidation.

～

This particular incident, though, was an unusual occurrence. Generally, flying itself holds no fears for me. It's getting on and off the planes that has become intolerable. The queues at check-in counters get longer and move more slowly; the amount of what is euphemistically described as 'hand luggage' seems to get bulkier. Passengers already seated are regularly assaulted by the suitcases, surf boards and cartonned plasma screens of those struggling down the aisle, staggering under the burdens of their 'hand luggage', which they then stuff into the overhead lockers with varying degrees of success. Flying economy class involves, as one writer has put it, 'frustration, degradation, inconvenience, authoritarianism, squalor, claustrophobia, humiliation, frustration, despair and fear'. So much of travel is sheer hard work. Yet once on board and airborne, a glass of wine in hand, kapok clouds floating past the window, anticipation of one's destination quickening, the air traveller's frustrations are forgotten.

Air travel has, however, created the greatest form of class distinction humanity has ever known, that between the back and the front of the plane. The gulf between the economy class cabin and that of business and first class has become more and more pronounced. This discrepancy, between the discomfort of economy class flying and the luxury of the business and first class cabins, explains one of the most powerful urges in travel

– the desire to be upgraded. There is no feeling quite like that experienced by a prioritised and seated business class traveller, sipping champagne, smugly watching the economy passengers struggling through their cabin on the way to the rear of the plane, lugging their suitcases, surfboards and plasma screens with them. The difference between economy class and business class is akin to the difference between riding in a Volkswagen and a Rolls Royce, and this comfort abyss has led to designated economy class travellers going to ridiculous lengths to try to be upgraded.

A friend booked on a flight from Auckland to London hated travelling economy so much that he pleaded uncontrollable flatulence. The smell, he said at the check-in counter, was so bad that he couldn't sit close to anyone else. To avoid offending his fellow-travellers, my friend explained politely, he needed to be upgraded to business class, where the seats were wide enough apart for the odour of his farts to disperse. The ruse did not work, the check-in woman assigned him a seat at the very back of the plane, next to the toilet. I have studied people ahead of me at the check-in counter, grovelling and pleading to be upgraded: geriatric couples claiming that they're on their honeymoon, men and women claiming they're holders of royal honours or have extreme medical conditions. Mostly, I've also noticed, they're declined, not always politely. Upgrades usually happen when the traveller least expects it. Once I was upgraded, completely unexpectedly and for no obvious reason, when flying from Osaka to London. It was a wonderfully comfortable flight, apart from the party of five East End slobs who celebrated their elevated status by drinking themselves stupid all the way, upsetting the demure Japanese air hostesses who had to serve them.

That's another thing about business class, it's no guarantee of classy behaviour.

Next to me in business class, bound for Sydney, is a middle-aged property developer from Baltimore. He's undone his shirt buttons, taken his shoes off, extricated his TV set from inside the armrest and tipped his seat well back to watch a movie. But the screen evidently has smears on it, because the man extends his socked right foot, wipes the TV vigorously with it, then does the same with his left foot. Like a gibbon. Then, seeing me watching him, he turns and snarls. 'Fucking dirty TV screen, you don't expect that in the front of the plane.'

Then there was the white South African man I once saw on an economy class trip, who was assigned a seat next to a Fijian man. The South African stood in the aisle, staring in disgust at his fellow-passenger, then turned to the hostess. 'You've put me next to a blek man. I refuse to sit next to 'eem. I want an upgrade, I *demand* an upgrade.' The hostess, a brunette of about 25, nodded thoughtfully. 'I'll have to talk to the In-flight Service Director about it,' she said, and went away. The complainant kept standing. I watched his face, detesting his superior expression. The Fijian man was frowning deeply, staring straight ahead, his lips puckered. Insulted. The hostess returned and nodded briskly at the South African. 'Right Sir, that's all sorted out,' she said, courteously. Then she gestured to the Fijian man. 'Mr Vinaka, would you like to follow me? We've a seat for you in business class.'

To be upgraded is a blissful experience, making it very difficult to return to the back end of the plane. But there are worse things. On a recent flight to Tahiti, I reported to check-in, and as I was involved in a travel writing assignment, requested if it was possible to be upgraded. The woman listened to my request, tapped her keyboard, frowned, picked up the phone. *Always a promising sign.* Replacing the phone, she nodded. 'Yes Mr Lay, there is space available.' The printer whirred, she handed the boarding pass over. 'Seat 6C.' Euphoria. Floating on air even though take-off was two hours away, I was admitted to the plush airline lounge, snacked there on cheese and biscuits, read the *Bulletin*, used the Internet facility, and when called, reported to the departure area. There, I began to feel alarmed. There was a big crowd waiting: crying children, frazzled parents, bickering couples. The flight was obviously going to be full. But still, I had my magic pass, the one for seat 6C. Minutes passed. Then an announcement came from the desk by the gate. 'Could Mr Lay report to the desk, please.' *Not a good sign.*

The man looked up, sighing. He was obviously under stress. 'Your boarding pass, please Mr Lay?' I handed it over. The man tapped his keyboard, looked up again. 'I'm afraid business class has been overbooked, Mr Lay, so I'll have to …'

I saw not just red, but crimson. Hell hath no fury like an upgraded passenger downgraded. Stepping forward, I said slowly, in a menacing tone, and through gritted teeth. 'Listen to me. Carefully.' I brought my face closer to his. 'I was given seat 6C and that's where I'll be sitting. If you don't put me in that business class seat I'll go straight down to the office of your airline and let your manager know that you've …'

The man thrust up his hands in a gesture of surrender. 'Please, please Mr Lay, let me finish.' He clicked his tongue. 'I was *going on* to say, that because business class is full, we've put you in first class instead.' He gave me a sardonic look. 'I presume you're not going to complain about *that* …'

First class. Not just French champagne, but *vintage* French champagne. The food was divine, too. And I was seated next to an elderly Hollywood movie producer and his 30-something Croatian wife. They were interesting company. Naturally, I pressed upon the producer three of my unsold books, along with my business card, but no subsequent film offer appeared.

It's difficult to exaggerate the difference air travel has made to people's lives. This applies in particular to those living on remote islands. Before airstrips were built throughout the Pacific – some of them constructed for strategic reasons during World War II – people relied on small inter-island trading vessels to get them from one island to another. These boats were slow and uncomfortable, their timetables erratic. Passengers shared the decks with cargo, live animals and poultry. Medical emergencies on isolated islands where facilities were inadequate meant that treatment was often fatally delayed.

The building of runways on far-flung islands changed all that. For instance, since an airstrip was completed on far-away Pukapuka atoll in 1994, it's been possible to fly from there to Rarotonga, the primary island of the Cook Islands, in three hours. Before that it took several days in a rusting, wallowing, puke-inducing tramp steamer. Air links such as the Rarotonga-Pukapuka connection have changed the island people's lives drastically. It's now such a simple matter to get to the atoll by air, and a simple matter to leave. Two other atolls in the northern group of the Cook Islands – Manihiki and Penrhyn – are linked to Rarotonga by a regular air service.

In engineering terms, building a runway on an atoll is relatively easy, much more straightforward than building one on a mountainous island. An atoll is an ancient, sunken volcano, with a central lagoon surrounded by long narrow islets of coral rock. On these slender strips of land there is no soil, neither are there any streams or rivers. The climate is arid, so fresh water is precious. Because the long narrow motus are only a couple of metres above the level of the surrounding ocean, from wherever you are on an atoll, the whole world appears to be flat. And with sufficient capital, earth-moving machinery and concrete making facilities, a runway can be laid out on a selected motu. Surveyors and engineers do the rest. The airstrip's built, a terminal and safety features are added, and you're ready to come and go. Runways have been grafted onto many of the atolls of the South Pacific, changing the people's way of life forever.

No island group is better served by air connections than the Tuamotu Archipelago, in French Polynesia, a constellation of 76 atolls scattered over 20,000 square kilometres of ocean. Over the last 40 years, the French government has poured billions of dollars into the atolls' infrastructure, initially for strategic reasons, to serve the former nuclear testing sites on Mururoa and Fangataufa atolls. Neighbouring Hao atoll too was a military base. In the 1980s and '90s, French airforce planes could be seen taking off and landing from Fa'a Airport, in Tahiti, bound for the atolls day and night. Now, mercifully, the French nuclear tests are over. Other atolls in the Tuamotus, such as Tikehau, also had runways built so that fish caught in their lagoons could be flown quickly from the island to the markets in Papeete, and scuba divers and tourists could be brought in.

Study a map of the Tuamotu Archipelago and you will see, superimposed on the scattered specks of coral, a score of aeroplane symbols, indicating that these are the atolls with runways, bringing them within an hour's flight of Tahiti.

I was invited to go to Fakarava atoll, in the Tuamotus. I rang a friend to let him know.

'I'm going to Fakarava,' I said.

'You're going to fuck a *what*?'

'A rava. I mean, that's a place. Faka-rava.'

'Oh. Where the hell is it?'

The Air Tahiti ATR 42 begins its descent, the features of Fakarava come into focus. The atoll's pale blue, roughly rectangular lagoon is huge, its floor mottled with pink coral heads. I glimpse a wide pass through the reef at the northern end, then a long line of motus, tapering far away to the south. Below us the runway is lined up, grey tarmac lined on both sides with dazzlingly white coral sand, scrubby vegetation and wavy palms, and the narrow island rushes up to meet us. I step out of the plane, into the superheated air of an atoll afternoon, walk over to the terminal and search the waiting crowd for someone called Ngahina.

A young woman steps forward, a frangipani garland in hand. 'M'sieur Gray-em?'

'Oui.'

She places the flowers around my neck. 'Je m'appelle Ngahina. Bienvenue a Fakarava.'

She is part-French, part-Tuamotuan, aged about 30. Slim, with large brown eyes, an oval face. Her long hair is dyed a gingery shade, she wears jeans and a skimpy white top, and around her neck is an ornate silver necklace with several clusters of black pearls attached to it. We pile into her ute outside the little terminal, then drive off down the motu.

Fakarava's lagoon is so wide − over 20 kilometres across − that at this level it's not possible to see the motus on its far side. The lagoon is like a sea within an ocean. The 40km-long eastern side of the atoll shrinks away to the horizon, so that the crowns of its distant coconut palms appear to be growing straight from the water. The lagoon itself is the sheerest, most intense shade of blue imaginable, dazzlingly, blindingly blue.

We drive into the atoll's main village, Rotoava. Here I see a handsome white Catholic church, a dive centre, a couple of stores, a snack bar, an infirmary, a few small houses, and that's it. But the village is immaculate. No graffiti, no litter, no signage. When I comment on this, Ngahina nods, 'The people on this island take great pride in their commune.' It shows.

I'm staying at a pension a few kilometres further down the motu run by Ngahina and her Mama, Flora. Flora is 60, a bronzed, wiry woman with a ready smile, dressed in a pink halter-top, floral shorts and jandals. She too is part-European, Danish in her case, and speaks little English. She shows me over the pension, called Tokerau Village. It consists of half a dozen spacious, comfortable bungalows on the inner edge of the lagoon, surrounded by gardens. Because atolls have only rubbly coral soil, it's hard work creating and maintaining any sort of garden, but

Flora has done a great job. Flowering shrubs, brilliantly blooming bougainvillea in particular, light up the garden, and there are also plantings of drought-resistant mossy grass. Adding another element to the garden are large pieces of bleached, contorted driftwood, which resemble abstract sculptures.

When I compliment Flora on her garden, she laughs. 'Yes, I have green hands.' Then: 'Pardon, I mean, green *fingers*.' Certainly, she works very hard at it, making compost from food scraps to feed her plants and saving the little rain that falls. A constant gardener. And on an atoll, everything that can be recycled is recycled. So all of Flora's gardens are bordered by lines of upside-down Heineken bottles, emptied by her thirsty guests. The bottles are arranged in wavy lines in the dazzlingly white coral sand. Green bottle borders, a green-fingered gardener. So her name, Flora Bordes, is perfect.

I snorkel at the bottom of the garden. Drifting near the surface of the lagoon, I watch a huge shoal of golden-eyed, mullet-like fish swim past, looking at me with indifference. Then I paddle the pension's kayak down the lagoon to the atoll's black pearl farm, pretending I'm Paul Theroux, and paddle back again. I take a shower by the jetty, then head off down the road on the pension bike, bound for Rotoava village. It's 33 degrees Celsius, but the trade wind is blowing straight off the ocean to my right, providing some relief.

The atoll's one road is amazing, running as it does right down the centre of the motu, dark and flat, like a licorice strap. I bike on. It's smoothly sealed and very wide, stretching away to the horizon. A boy racer's dream. Thankfully there are none here. I pedal harder, my thigh muscles protesting. But it's such a wonderful road. There are marked cycle lanes on either side, but so little traffic that I can ignore them and stay in the middle. After biking for half an hour, I'm overtaken by one small truck and two motor-bikes. Only 699 people live on Fakarava, so I wonder at the need for such a magnificent road here. It's so straight and beautifully formed, and as wide as a runway. It must have cost millions to build. You could land a 747 on it. *Wide as a runway. Land a 747.* The centime drops. That must be it, that's what the road was intended for, built by the French in case of a military emergency. In which case the Fakarava road could be used as a stationary aircraft carrier. Such a horrible thought that I shake it away and instead concentrate on the horizon.

Pedalling on, I pass several other pensions and Fakarava's one resort hotel, the Maitai. I come across a snack bar – Snack Elda – where I stop for lunch. Run by a large Marquesan woman, presumably Elda, it's fairly basic, but it serves me a chicken chow mein that is so big I can't finish it. Outside the snack bar, under the palm trees beside the lagoon, a group of nuns in dark blue habits is lunching too. Fakarava is a very Catholic atoll, the Mormons apparently having not yet put the island on their proselytising programme.

In Rotoava village I wander about the small dock, check out the yachts anchored in the lee of the atoll and again wonder at the size of Fakarava's lagoon and its infinite blue beauty. Late in 2006 Fakarava was added to UNESCO's Man and Biosphere (MAB) programme, a global list of places of exceptional environmental purity where local communities are actively involved in their conservation. This is indeed a commune that cares.

Across the water, the highest object in sight is a tiered stone lighthouse, built in the 1950s to warn approaching vessels of the coral hazards ahead. Atolls are so close to sea level that for years they posed perils for sailing ships at night; you only knew you were near land when you hit it.

Back at the pension, I come across Flora fertilising her plants. She looks up and smiles. 'Did you enjoy your chicken chow mein at Snack Elda?' she asks. It must be hard to keep a secret on an atoll.

That night Flora and Ngahina and I sit around the dinner table and with the aid of my French-English-French phrase book, we enjoy a long conversation. Like most Tahitian people, Flora and Ngahina are fascinated by New Zealand Maori culture, its ancestral connections and similarities to theirs. The Tuamotuan language, local observers and philologists alike say, is very similar to New Zealand Maori. Flora proudly shows me a New Zealand calendar she bought while on holiday in Auckland last year. Each month has a Maori design – a koru, a patu, a whale's tail – and both women are captivated by these emblems and their symbolism. So much so that Ngahina, who makes jewellery using black pearls farmed in Fakarava's lagoon, has blended some of the Maori motifs into her designs. I ask Flora where she stayed when she visited Auckland. 'Sky Ceety,' she replies, her face lighting up at the memory. 'La Tour du Ciel, c'est merveilleux!'

Ngahina and Flora drive me to the airport for the 40-minute return flight to Tahiti. At the airport I'm checked in by a solidly built, affable, distinctly effeminate man of about 50 with orange bougainvillea flowers in his wispy hair. 'My uncle,' Ngahina murmurs to me. Then a pretty girl in an Air Tahiti uniform hands me my boarding pass. Ngahina introduces me. 'This is Leah. My cousin.' We wander over to the terminal's Le Snack for a sandwich. As the woman behind the counter serves us, Ngahina introduces me to her too. 'My aunty,' explains Ngahina. By now I'm getting the hang of the place. So when a burly man in a police uniform approaches, plants a gentle kiss on each of Ngahina's cheeks, then shakes my hand before moving away, I say: 'I'll bet he's your uncle.'

Ngahina blinks. 'No, he must be new here. I've never seen him before.'

The plane soars into the blue, outstripping wisps of cloud. And there below is Fakarava, its endless line of motu, its wave-dashed reef, its vast lagoon, its mop-topped palms. A sight that could never be appreciated in the same way at sea level.

Air travel, there's nothing in the world like it.

Looking ahead, 'aviation futurists' (yes, there are such people) predict that jetliners will commonly have a passenger capacity of over 600. Already such a plane – the Airbus 380 – is in production. It has twin passenger decks running the full length of its fuselage, a take-off weight of 1.235 million pounds and it will carry 555 passengers. (The trouble with the Airbus 380 project, however, is that it's now beset with financial and technical problems. So serious are these problems that this particular giant plane may never fly commercially.) The giant planes of the near future will need much larger engines, longer wingspans, extended runways, wider taxiways and passing zones as they trundle along the ground. Thus the demand for suitable land for runways and terminals will increase dramatically, although vertical take off and landing aircraft will save some space. But whichever way you look at it, the world's skies will be filled with more and more planes and more and more air travellers.

As for what all those engine emissions will be contributing to global warming, that's another story.

# The Train Traveller

London to Paris by train – I had seldom looked forward to a journey so much. After all, the line goes through the Channel Tunnel, one of the modern world's great engineering feats. I had often stood on top of the chalk cliffs above Dover or Eastbourne, staring across at the cliffs on the French coast, their geological twins. To travel by train directly beneath the body of water that separated Britain and France had always appealed to me; I was ready to try the Chunnel.

It was at Waterloo in 1815 that the English inflicted their heaviest defeat on their traditional foe, the French. It is tempting to wonder if the English choice of Waterloo Station as the London terminus of the Eurorail connection between there and Paris was made with history in mind. Presumably the French were consulted.

Joined to one side of the massive Victorian Waterloo Station, on the south side of the Thames, is the ultra-modern terminal for Eurostar, the brand name for the high speed passenger trains which have connected London with Paris, Brussels and

Amsterdam since 1994. The Eurostar terminal is covered with a stretched grey canopy supported by an exposed framework of blue tubular steel. Transparent, well lit and emphatically post-modern, the terminal contrasts starkly with the dank, forbidding Victorian station alongside it. But what excites me most as I pass into the upper level of the building is what I can see just on the other side of the transparent walls: train engines, three of them, at the very end of the line. Train engines like no others I have ever seen; yellow and white, sleek, modern, their snouts raked back at a sharp angle, resembling a row of moray eels in an aquarium. These are the Eurostar engines, ready and waiting to go.

Check-in time is 20 minutes before departure. I approach a row of stainless steel machines. Passengers slip their tickets into one of the machines, as if they were going no further than from Piccadilly Circus to Leicester Square, and the machine reads it and shoots it back. The approved traveller then passes through a chrome turnstile and into the rail terminal.

It is a relief to turn my back on the grime and litter of old Waterloo and move through into the new. Just as passing through to the 'airside' at an international airport is to enter a sealed and suspended world, so too does moving through to 'railside' at Waterloo have an ethereal aspect to it.

The modernistic departure lounge has been designed to resemble a gigantic railway carriage, with a décor of grey carpet and red leather seats. It's like stepping straight into Europe. The tannoy announcements are in French and English, the lounge is lined with Euro-boutiques, duty-free shops, bureaux de change and gift stores selling Eurostar caps, T-shirts and jackets. There is also a last stand of English gourmet food: a delicatessen selling smoked Scottish farmed salmon for $100 a fillet, a jar of Stilton cheese for $40, as well as Beluga caviar for $1000. The waiting French, Belgian and German passengers are easily distinguishable from the English. The English are dowdy, the others are Europeans. There's also a surprisingly large number of Japanese waiting to board the train.

Fifteen minutes to my 9.53am departure. I change my English pounds into euros at a bureau de change, then wander about. It's crowded in here, but plush and very comfortable, and an electronic information board that heightens the imminence of departure. But where have the trains gone? There's not a carriage or an engine in sight. Departure 9016 is flashing on the board, but where is the train itself? Ah, *je comprends*. The platforms are on an upper level, and over there is an escalator ...

Up the escalator and there at the top, by the platform, waiting and ready, is Eurostar 9016, just below the canopy roof. I find my carriage – Number 7 – enter, take my seat.

When I was a boy, train travel was a cruel and common punishment. The New Zealand Railway trains were slow, smelly and comfortless. Any part of the carriage's interior that you touched left you with grime on your hands and clothes. And the rail system seemed to be staffed entirely by the retarded. Going by rail from Taranaki to Wellington was such a squalid experience that for a long time I vowed that I would never again go anywhere by train.

But this train is light years away from that New Zealand train experience of the 1960s. It is carpeted in diagonal stripes: variegated greys and burnt-orange. Even the ceiling is carpeted. The seat is wide and accommodating, it reclines and there is an adjustable foot-rest. There is a tray table in front of me, and ample space in the overhead locker when I stow my jacket and pack. Smoking is *defense*. Out of habit I reach for a seat belt, this is so much like the interior of an Airbus or a 777, but much less cramped. Already, I like this train.

Other people enter and take their seats. Opposite me is a cockney couple dressed in their best casuals, giving themselves a weekend in Paris for a wedding anniversary treat, perhaps. A little way along is a young English couple, a brother and sister I guess, she about 25, he perhaps 18. She is tall and strapping, with long blonde hair and buck teeth; he has a smooth round face and a shaven head. She has with her the largest backpack I've ever seen: green, bulging and big enough to contain several parachutes and platoon provisions for a D-Day landing. When she turns in the aisle the pack nearly knocks the other passengers flying.

The boy has no pack and sports the two of the severest black eyes I've ever seen. The bruising spreads out over his cheekbones and laterally almost to his ears. Whatever inflicted this grievous injury (his sister's backpack, perhaps?) did not confine itself to his face – the three middle fingers of his left hand are strapped with white tape, obliging him to hold them up in the air like someone making a rude gesture. But before the train moves off, both are sleeping like Hansel and Gretel.

In front of me a businessman is already tapping his laptop, having spared himself the ordeal of getting out to Heathrow or Gatwick and queuing at the check-in counter. As I have already been reminded by those converted to surface travel, avoiding all that makes for priceless savings in time and blood pressure. Trains, these people aver, are the civilised way to go.

On the stroke of 9.53am Eurostar 9016 glides off on its wide gauge tracks, out of Waterloo and, already at a quickening pace, through the suburbs of South London under a streaky January sky. I feel another tremor of excitement pass through me, the thrill of a long-anticipated journey at last commenced.

SOME FACTS:
- circa 10,000 years ago: the end of the Ice Age and consequent rising sea levels cut though the soft chalk strata connecting Britain to the continent of Europe, creating a natural moat. For centuries people on both sides of the moat dreamed of again connecting the detached lands, so that they

could travel across it as easily as their prehistoric ancestors had before being cut off by the sea. The last time Britain was successfully invaded from Europe was in 1066AD.

• September 1981: France and the United Kingdom announce the launch of studies of the feasibility of a fixed link under the channel.

• December 1987: Channel tunnel construction begins.

• June 1991: tunnel boring is complete.

• May 1994: inauguration of the tunnel by Queen Elizabeth II of England and President Francois Mitterand of France.

• November 1994: first Eurostar commercial services begin from London, Paris and Brussels. Travel time from central London to central Paris is three hours.

• March 1997: the nine millionth passenger travels by Eurostar.

• December 1997: opening of the Belgian High Speed Line reduces London-Brussels time to two hours, 40 minutes.

• July 2003: a Eurostar train set a new UK rail speed record of 334.7kph (208mph) during safety testing on the first section of the Channel Tunnel Rail Link (CTRL). This section opened for commercial services in September 2003.

• September 2004: Eurostar carriages' interiors are refurbished.

• 2007: completion of the second phase of the Channel Tunnel Rail Link (CTRL), standardising the English, French and Belgian rail lines. Eight trains per hour in each direction are able to travel from London's new Eurorail station to the Continent.

～

10.25 am. The rows of dull brick and chimney-topped suburban houses have slipped behind us, we're now into England's green and pleasant land. We're on the standard Waterloo-Ashford-Folkestone line that slashes across Kent. The train is already moving so swiftly that it isn't possible to read the names on the local stations as they flash by, but within the carriage there is no real sensation of speed. The train runs so smoothly that it is like flying on rails. There is just a very slightly tremulous, ever-so-gentle rocking motion to suggest the extreme velocity.

SOME TECHNICAL FACTS:
• The trains derived from the fundamental mechanical features of the innovative, highly successful French TGV. Each Eurostar train is nearly 400 metres long and carries 750 passengers in 18 carriages.

• The trains weigh 752.4 tonnes and are fitted with 12 asynchronous electrical traction motors, giving a total output of 16,408 hp – the equivalent of 20 Formula 1 racing cars. Each train costs $70 million.

• In case of an 'incident' in the Channel Tunnel, the trains can be divided in order to evacuate the passengers in the unaffected carriages.

The train glides on through the velvet pastures and soggy lowlands of the Weald, in Kent. The ploughed fields lie dark and open, like trays of cooked mince, the trees are filigreed silhouettes against the pale grey sky. Bare fruit trees flash by, along with gingerbread-shingled, white weatherboard farmhouses and Kentish oasthouses, their cones capped with white like KKK hats.

The in-train service is French. There are dashing French stewards and lovely French stewardesses, there is French food, French beer, French wine. Not a stuffed baked potato or a spotted dick in sight. Guy, a personable young Parisian with close-cropped black hair, places a warm roll in front of me. 'How fast are we going?' I ask him.

'Here in England, only one hundred and sixty kilometres per hour. Here the track is not so straight. But after we get to France, three hundred kilometres per hour!' He grins triumphantly. 'The track is better in France, we can go much faster on the other side.'

Ashford, an otherwise nondescript town in Kent, has for the last decade been an international rail node. Here the train stops briefly, and from now on the peace in the carriage is shattered, for at Ashford a very county couple, Mr and Mrs Hathorn-Topiary, join the train and their allocated seats are just behind mine.

He is tall and long-faced, with wisps of grey hair gelled against his lumpy scalp; she is haggard, with lifeless blonde hair and a disagreeable mouth. They are in their late 50s, and their accents are very upper middle-class, their voices braying. And very soon after resuming our journey, the entire company of carriage seven is aware of the Hathorn-Topiary's domestic difficulties.

Mr H-T: 'I simply can't manage without a reversing light. I can't *imagine* why Citroen makes the CV108 without a reversing light. I mean, you *know* how long our driveway is, don't you?'

Mrs H-T: 'Yus, yus. *I* can't manage without a reversing light, either. Let's go back to Rover. Oh, more chardonnay here, *garçon*.'

Mr H-T: 'Rover, yairs. We should never have not bought British in the first place. I think a Rover, yairs. Mind you, they're owned by BMW now.'

Mrs H-T: 'Are they? *Are they?*'

Mr H-T: 'Yairs, dammit. Mind you, as a shareholder in

Rover ...'

Mrs H-T: 'A small shareholder ...'

Mr H-T: 'Yairs.'

Mrs H-T: (holding out her glass for more chardonnay) 'But you still ought to be entitled to a discount. On a Rover.'

Even the Hathorn-Topiaries are silenced by the impending significance of the next stage of our journey. The train slows, we begin a just-discernible descent and I glimpse the depot between Dover and Folkestone, where those travelling by car drive their vehicles onto special carriages. Seconds later there is a dip into darkness.

It is warm in the Chunnel and rather airless. My ears begin to pop in the pressurised atmosphere. This would be a claustrophobe's nightmare. No one in the carriage is speaking now. I imagine we are all thinking the same thing: that just above our heads in England's moat, the Channel, La Manche, countless tonnes of chalk strata, sand, sea water, along with many ships and their weighty cargoes, are bearing down on the Chunnel roof. And as if to emphasise this fact, there is also a strange rushing sound in the carriage, a disconcertingly wave-like sound, like the one you hear when you hold a shell to your ear. Where does this sound come from? Could it really be the sea?

Outside the carriage there is only the occasional streaked light, everything else is blackness. In this strange, ethereal atmosphere, Eurostar 9016 glides silently on. Then, less than 20 minutes later, there is a little light at the end of the tunnel, and with breathtaking suddenness we pop out into France.

Wide, undulating farm landscapes, misty at the margins. Copses of skeletal trees, cars on the wrong side of the roads, village houses clumped together, church spires rising from their centres like sharpened pencils.

Guy the steward pauses beside me and considerately slips a paper coaster under the glass of wine on my tray table. 'Sometimes the glass can slide,' he explains, 'when we go at top speed.' A postprandial serenity has settled over the carriage. People doze. From behind me, I can hear the soft snores of Mr and Mrs Hathorn-Topiary. The rest is silence.

But I don't want to sleep, I want to watch everything in sight. *France, I'm in France.* There is a motorway beside the Eurorail track. The Peugeots, Citroens and Renaults on the autoroute must be going at about 130km per hour, but Eurostar makes the cars seem as if they're in low gear. Now we're flying even faster, yet still there is little sensation of speed. The train merely sways a little, which it is entitled to do at 300km per hour. Eurostar slides through the fields of Picardy like a steel snake, devouring the kilometres greedily.

And it's right, I think, what the rail converts say: this leaves travelling by air between London and Paris for dead. I can get up, walk about, use a mobile phone, have a good wash, see where I'm going. There is an at-seat trolley service. If I were a baby I could have my bottle warmed; as a grown-up I can have my chardonnay chilled.

Hamlets, villages, ploughed fields, vast and open to the continental sky, laid bare for planting. A rainbow arcs over the open land. The French countryside has a bleak, silent beauty. We pass a gently sloping hillside, and there is a small square cemetery with rows of identical white crosses and a tricolour flying from a mast in the cemetery's centre. A few seconds later there is another little cemetery, then another, reminders that this part of France was once a human slaughterhouse.

I remember with a jolt that my great-uncle, a country lad from the Rangitikei, an officer in the New Zealand Medical Corps, was killed out there. On 18 July 1918, just four months before the Armistice. William Ingle, I wonder, which cross is yours?

And that prompts another thought: the train has not paused for frontier formalities. These days Europeans move with complete ease across national boundaries. A passport has become virtually unnecessary for members of the European

Union who do not wish to leave Europe. But what about non-Europeans? A New Zealander, for example. What is to stop him jumping onto Eurostar, sneaking into France and staying there? And as if the authorities have overheard my thought, there is a bilingual announcement: passport checks will be made on board and officials will be moving through the train shortly to carry out these formalities. This is done without fuss or complication, in a matter of minutes, and shortly afterwards, glancing up ahead at the horizon, I can see an instantly recognisable landmark, the Eiffel Tower. From London to Paris has taken just two hours and 35 minutes. Too soon, too soon. I could stay on this train all week.

Paris, for no logical reason, is one hour ahead of London time. By the time we have advanced our watches we are passing through the messy, strife-torn banlieues of the city of light. Five minutes later and we are within the vast confines of Gare du Nord station.

Paris. What can I write that hasn't already been written about this city? What writer has not extolled it for centuries? What else can I think except that if it looks this good in mid-winter, what must it be like in spring?

But I do discover something that I was not aware of on earlier visits, when I was travelling by car: the heart of Paris is best and most easily explored on foot. It is a compact city, and the Seine's bridges are much closer together than London's. There are also small, comfortable hotels for reasonable prices on both banks. I'm staying in one just behind the Louvre. Tall and skinny, it looks like something out of *Irma La Douce*, and to my delight the owner explains that indeed it was once a brothel. It has an ancient, clanking lift, narrow passages and a view over the city's grey rooftops. Just down the street is a bronze statue of the playwright Molière (1622–1673).

The rest of Paris is virtually on my doorstep: the Louvre, Notre Dame, the Champs-Elysées, St Germain, the antiquarian bookstalls and the cafés, canopied in clear plastic against the cold.

The city is a walker's treat. On my right is the Left Bank, on my left is the Right Bank.

And Paris is indeed the city of love. Everywhere I see couples: holding hands, embracing, kissing, hugging, unselfconsciously, delightfully.

As I'm strolling beside the Seine in the crisp twilight I see yet another such couple down on the riverside path, each wearing a long black winter coat. They are clutching each other and kissing. It is a scene of such romantic perfection, so utterly Parisian, that I can't resist walking down the steps to get closer to them. I walk down, approach, pretend I'm looking at the riverboats. But like all lovers, they have eyes only for one another. As I get closer, their mouths unlock and they draw apart, but continue to gaze into each other's eyes, enraptured. I get closer still, then stop, startled. They are both in their early twenties, both very beautiful. And both are women.

I walk on, reach the Louvre, stroll past the shops under the colonnades of the Rue Tivoli, buy a black beret and pretend I'm a Frenchman – till I realise I'm the only man in Paris wearing one – and buy hot chestnuts from a man roasting them on a brazier. Gypsy women with rotting teeth and ragged shawls hold their grubby babies up to me imploringly. Averting my eyes guiltily, I walk on into the beautiful, octagonal Place Vendôme, past the opulent boutiques and the Ritz entrance, where Diana and Dodi made their last exit. As I walk across the Place, soft snowflakes begin to drift down across the city.

Before the end of the weekend I find myself wanting to be back on the train. On Sunday afternoon I take le Metro back to the Gare du Nord. There my train is waiting, its engines already throbbing, and half an hour later I'm again flying on rails through Picardy. Eurostar's great advantage is its speed. It is also its disadvantage. On the trip back, I have the same overriding feeling: I don't want to get off this train. At just two hours and 35 minutes, the pleasure is far too fleeting. As Sydney Carton might have mused in Dickens' *A Tale of Two Cities*, had he gone to the guillotine by Eurostar: 'It was the best of trains, it was the best of trains.'

A FINAL FACT:

- In August 2006 the company which runs the Eurotunnel was adjudged to be $NZ18,000,000,000 in debt.

# The Day Traveller

Getting from one place to another today is ridiculously easy. Distance has been shrivelled to insignificance. Londoners fly to New York and arrive earlier than when they left; many Aucklanders commute to Sydney. From London, you can go to Paris or Brussels for lunch. I've been to Holland eight times and never once spent the night there. So when I was offered the chance to go to China for the day, from Hong Kong, I didn't hesitate.

I say China, but in fact my destination was Shenzhen, a city just across the border from Hong Kong's New Territories, in Guangdong province. The latter is China's richest region.

Twenty-five years ago, Shenzhen was a village housing mainly peasant farmers. Then, in what must be one of the most astonishingly rapid economic transformations in history, the village was turned into a metropolis. Shenzhen had been classified as one of China's 'Special Economic Zones', and the command economy yielded almost overnight to laissez-faire capitalism, where anything goes as long as it makes money. And everything went. Shenzhen boomed. Rice paddies and vegetable plots were turned into industrial estates and golf courses, village houses were replaced by apartment blocks and in the centre of Shenzhen dozens of high-rise office towers were built. The peasant farmers who had owned the land became overnight multi-millionaires who invested in more industrial estates, golf courses, luxury hotels and high-rise office towers. At the last count there were 15 billionaires in China and the number is rising fast. One of them, the world's wealthiest self-made woman, Zhang Yin, comes from Shenzhen. Worth $US5.08 billion, middle-aged Zhang made her fortune from recycling scrap paper bought from the US. The scrap paper is shipped back to China and turned into containerboard at Zhang's factories in southern and eastern China, earning her the unique honorific 'Empress of Waste Paper'.

As the coach whirled me and my tour party – mostly holidaying Malays and Indians from Kuala Lumpur – around Shenzhen's ring road, I couldn't take my eyes off the cluster of glass and steel towers in the distance. So high, so modern, so glittering that they resembled virtual reality rather than reality itself, like a computer-generated city. Hundreds of storeys high, the surreal towers pierced the grey South China sky, their pale green glass exteriors resembling something from a Brick Bradford sci-fi comic of the 1930s. The silhouettes of cranes could also be seen, helping to build yet more towers as communism was obliterated and consumerism triumphed.

My mind boggled at the drive, energy and ambition behind all this, and the Chinese genius for creating wealth from almost nothing. For the first time I was witnessing one of the sources of the plasma screens, weedeaters, laptops and printers, mobile phones, garden tools, toys, baseball caps, shirts, socks and sneakers which are pouring out from the industrial estates of China and into the western world's shopping malls.

I would have liked to have seen more of the commercial core of Shenzhen, but this wasn't possible. Time was short. I was on a fixed itinerary, one-day tour. This morning we were going to something called 'Shenzhen Window of the World', followed by lunch at one of the city's luxury hotels, then in the afternoon we were being whisked off to the China Folk Culture Village.

Accordingly, a few minutes later, the coach drew up outside Shenzhen Window of the World. Two hours later, I had seen the wonders of the entire world. Angkor Wat of Cambodia, the Eiffel Tower, the Leaning Tower of Pisa, the Tower of London, the Pyramids of Giza, the Sphinx, the Acropolis of Athens and the Colosseum of Rome are all replicated on various scales: 1:1, 1:5 or 1:15. Where once there was a rice paddy there is now the Mahamuni Pagoda of Rangoon; where there had been a duck farm there is now Manhattan Island. The Acropolis and the statue of Buddha (the one which the fanatical Afghan Taleban blew up) are replicated on a scale of 1:1, the Pagoda 1:15. There are temples from Kyoto and pagodas from Bangkok, all set among miniature forests, lakes and bamboo groves. And apart from the obviously reduced size of the world's wonders, they have every appearance of reality. The Sphinx is suitably distressed; the Leaning Tower inclines at just the right angle. The Great Wall of China follows the ridges of the hills throughout the park, complete with a sentry post atop each rise. What in theory is a tacky, even exploitive concept is actually very, very interesting. The only thing spoiling the illusion is the sight of Shenzhen's high-rise apartments, rising from the ground beyond the park's perimeter, and the scarlet advertising signs of the multi-national corporations that have found economic advantages in the city.

I wander about this rambling, apparently endless theme park in the company of a middle-aged Malaysian law lecturer, Junid Saham, who is also travelling alone. Junid is a thoughtful, quietly spoken man, and I'm finding his company agreeable. We stroll about the park, marvelling at the apparent authenticity of these ersatz wonders of the world, this example of cultural appropriation on a global scale. We peer over Niagara Falls and stand on the brink of the Grand Canyon, traverse a tropical rainforest in a cable car, but baulk at taking a run on skis at the indoor piste. Whoever dreamed up this idea, I wonder; an ex-peasant farmer who could see that Shenzhen was going to be over-supplied with golf courses? A group of former duck farmers who dreamed of making over the world and whose entrepreneurial genius was liberated by the creation of the Special Economic Zone? Whoever it was, he or they had saved me years of travel and thousands of dollars, for in just two hours I am able to take in the entire cultural and natural wonders of the ancient and modern world. Junid reflects as we climb back onto the coach, with the Eiffel Tower still visible over the high fence surrounding the park, 'Now I can tell my children I have walked all the way from Niagara Falls to Venice's canals, in just two hours.'

We lunch with the rest of the tour party in the dining room of a huge, extremely vulgar hotel (gold Grecian columns, spouting dolphin fountains, cavorting marble nymphs), all sitting around a large round table with a lazy-Susan buffet rotating clockwise before us. I use a fork, Junid eats holding his chopsticks in his left hand. I notice the other Asian members of our party glancing at him, frowning, then looking away. After a time Junid says to me quietly, out of the side of his mouth, 'It's because I'm left-handed. In this part of the world the left hand is traditionally used to wipe one's arse.' I gulp. How embarrassing. But Junid is unfazed. Shrugging, he says, 'I can't help it if I was born left-handed.'

The afternoon is given over to the Chinese Folk Culture Village. Here again the world, or at least the Sino-World, has been compressed into an estate of several hectares. China is a nation of 56 ethnic groups, from the Buyi of Sichuan province to the yurt-dwelling people of Mongolia and scores of others in between. This park is all 1:1 in scale, thoroughly idealised and immaculate: the yurts are spotless, the streets swept, the temples perfect, the architecture exquisite. It's a spectacularly beautiful propaganda park. Camels and elephants with elegant covers wander through the park. There are live performances too, by young women in folk costume, singing to the accompaniment of stringed instruments. The dancers are exquisitely beautiful, if doll-like, in their diaphanous yellow gowns, their torsos and limbs swaying to the music. Falun Gong practitioners are not represented here, however.

The main problem now is that it is very, very hot. And it's tiring, walking around the recreated village streets. Seeing all the wonders of the world in the morning and all of China's ethnic groups in the afternoon is proving too much. After a couple of hours I can't take another temple, or traditional folk music group. The China Folk Culture Village comprises 200,000 square metres, and Junid and I have trudged around most of them. So after arranging to meet him again later in the Mongol-ethnic area, I creep away. In the Mongol area I come across a colourful yurt, one which is far too fancy for horseback-riding nomadic herdsmen and which looks as if it had been designed for Mongolian royalty. Looking inside, I see that it's beautifully decorated, its walls embroidered with pastoral scenes of the Mongolian steppes. Also, there's no one inside. And there's an irresistible-looking couch, covered with more multi-coloured, embroidered patterns. I lie down on it, and soon afterwards, fall into a heavy sleep. An hour later, I'm woken by an anxious Junid, shaking me by the shoulder. 'Graeme, wake up! The coach is leaving!'

Driving back to Hong Kong, we see hundreds of container lorries lined up, several lanes of them, at the crossing point between China and Hong Kong. The lorries are carrying goods produced in the factories of the Shenzen Special Economic Zone to the port of Hong Kong, for export to all parts of the world. It was supposed to be Napoleon Bonaparte who declared that 'China is a sleeping giant. When it awakes, the whole world will tremble'. The giant has awoken, and the world is indeed trembling before it. With the sheer weight of China's consumer goods.

# The Independent Traveller

The automobile is a much-maligned means of transport. We're told it's dirty, it's polluting, it clogs city streets, it kills pedestrians and people in other cars. Cars are bad for you is the nagging message.

Cars are also the most convenient form of personal transport ever invented. They allow people to travel long distances at reasonable cost and visit regions they could otherwise only dream of. It allows travellers to come and go exactly when they please. Only a car can take you (within reason) from the door of your place of departure to the door of your destination. Having a car permits travellers to make their own timetable, it gives them the independence to explore new regions at leisure. A car can be the traveller's best friend.

This is especially so in Australia, where everywhere is a very long way from everywhere else. Naturally you can fly from everywhere to everywhere, but you'll miss seeing in close-up all the interesting places in between.

Melbourne and Adelaide are 700km apart as the magpie

flies. You can fly between the capitals of Victoria and South Australia in an hour. You can take the Hamilton Highway – the inland road – and drive from one to the other in about ten hours. Or you can drive along the coast of Victoria into South Australia, taking the route known as the Great Ocean Road. This is the route I'm taking, driving a rental car, a near-new Nissan Pulsar. For some reason, the car has Queensland licence plates.

Melbourne's harbour, Port Phillip, is like a giant keyhole cut into the coast of Victoria. It takes a full hour's driving to put the towers and suburbs of Melbourne behind me and make my way around the keyhole to Geelong, then across the Bellarine Peninsula to the little town of Torquay, then on to Bells Beach. From here it's not far to the start of the Great Ocean Road, but as a one-time surfer I can't resist calling in to look at Bells Beach.

Bells Beach is to surfing what Lords is to cricket and Wimbledon is to tennis. The waves of Bells have helped make world champions. Parking areas and viewing platforms have been built along the crests of the cliffs, grandstands for viewing Bells' famous wave breaks. I park the car and walk to the nearest platform.

The cliff is about 20 metres high. Its top is edged with bonsai-sized vegetation, giving 180-degree views of Bass Strait. Today the water is like blue-green glass and the mottled rocks of the reef that extends from the base of the cliff are clearly visible. The waves appear first as long low mounds, a kilometre or so out in the strait. The mounds gradually swell and steepen, building into glassy walls which rear up, then hover, crests fluttering, before breaking and peeling away from the reef. They're not huge, the way they are in Oahu in Hawaii or Teahupoo in Tahiti, but they are perfectly formed. Today there are half a dozen riders down there, awaiting the right wave. When it comes the riders thrust themselves forward, then glide down the face of the glassy wall, ducking, swerving and pirouetting. It's enough to make an old surfer salivate, and I'm reluctant to tear myself away from the spectacle, but this is just the beginning. It's another 800km to my ultimate destination, Adelaide, and half of these kilometres will take me along the Great Ocean Road.

The road is aptly named. Alongside it is a great ocean, and it's a great road. Work began on building it in 1919, with labour provided by soldiers just returned from the battlefields of World War I. Diggers in every sense of the word, the ex-soldiers hewed the road into the coast's cliffs and headlands with picks, shovels and crowbars, developing it in sections. As they were completed the sections were opened as toll roads, then the tolls were abolished when the trust which had been set up to finance the project handed the road over to the Victorian State Government, on 2 October, 1936. There's a monument to the Herculean labours of the workers – a sturdy wooden arch across the road – at Eastern View, half an hour's drive west from Torquay.

Glancing at the map beside me I see that the coast here is like a series of sprockets bulging into Bass Strait, separated by deep bays. As far as the driving goes, the most obvious thing is the smoothness of the two-lane road and the lightness of the traffic. Heavy vehicles have to take the inland Hamilton Highway. And the other drivers here are considerate, exhibiting none of the impatience and aggression that to my mind characterises driving in New Zealand. The road winds around promontories, then levels out and passes alongside the blue satin sea and long empty beaches of golden sand.

My first stop is Apollo Bay, a holiday settlement tucked on the eastern side of the most prominent sprocket on the Victoria coast, Cape Otway. Apollo Bay is a small fishing port too, and after checking into a motel in the township, I think I'll go for a walk out to the harbour at the other end of the settlement to look at the fishing boats. But it's after five o'clock and as it's winter and there's a harsh chill in the sea air, I take the car instead.

From the boat harbour at Apollo Bay there's a fine view looking back at the curving beach and the bush-covered hills behind the town, but a holiday resort in winter, lacking people, always has a forlorn aspect, so I get back into the car. Then, looking up, I see a hotel on the headland above the harbour. In the fading light its line of glowing windows looks inviting, so I drive up, park the car, go inside and order a beer from the bar.

Again, the view looking back across the beach and town is attractive, and I imagine that in summer Apollo Bay must become a special place, lively and full of surprises.

'Another drink?' the barman asks, and I accept the offer.

He's a cordial chap, inquiring where I'm from and what I'm doing in Apollo Bay at the height of the off-season, and the second beer slips down quickly. The barman says, 'Another drink?' I'm about to say 'yes', when I look at the time. It's nearly six o'clock, I'm hungry, and I want to try one of the restaurants in the town. So I finish the drink I've got, say goodbye to the barman, get back into the car and drive down the hill and into the town's main street. The closed shops are on the left, the deserted beach on my right.

Half way along the street a blue-uniformed cop steps out from the row of parked cars. In one hand he holds a torch, in the other a device for detecting the presence of alcohol on a driver's breath. He holds up his torch hand, gesturing me to stop. I do, and in the long moment between seeing the policeman and halting the car, many thoughts – most of them self-reproving – race through my mind. *Why did I have that second drink? Why did I have that first drink? Why didn't I walk to the end of the town? How does a travel writer researching a driving story cope if he can't drive? It's a Monday night, what sort of a fool gets caught drink-driving on a Monday night?*

I stop the car and wind down the window. The cop is very tall and has to stoop to come close to the window. He's about 35, with a long, deeply creased face, grey eyes and big ears. It's an unmistakably Aussie face, a Chips Rafferty face. Squinting at me, he says gruffly, 'You drive here from Queensland?'

Briefly confused, I then remember the car's licence plates. 'No, no. I've just come from Melbourne. This is a rental car.' Flushed with embarrassment, I decide to come clean. 'Look officer, I've had a couple of drinks and I …'

The cop's big face comes closer. 'That right?' It's impossible to tell if the confession has helped my case or not. Probably not. His 'That right?' carried a note of heightened interest. He thrusts the breathaliser device in front of my face. 'Say your name and where you come from into this. Slowly.'

I do so, knowing that I'm condemning myself from my own lips. I breathe out, slowly. The cop takes the device away and looks at it closely. Now I've gone cold all over. Questions race through my brain. *Do they have instant fines in Victoria? If not, when will the court hearing be? Do I have enough cash to pay the fine? Can you pay a fine with a credit card? How will I get the car back to Melbourne airport?*

The cop bends down again, then says in a slow, amiable Aussie tone, 'No worries, mate. On yer way.'

I feel like getting out of the car and embracing him. But I don't. Instead I drive the 100 metres to my motel, pour myself a large glass of duty-free brandy and having been spared the humiliation of a court conviction, make a vow that I will never again let another glass of alcohol pass my lips before driving.

Cape Otway is also a national park. Covered in temperate rainforest, the cape is bisected by the Ocean Road, with a branch road leading out to the cape itself. This road passes through groves of identically contorted eucalyptus trees and ends at the beginning of a path to the Cape Otway lighthouse.

The lighthouse stands on the apex of the triangular cape, commanding a breath-sucking, wind-blasting view over the western entrance to Bass Strait. Bright white and shaped like a giant's salt cellar, the lighthouse was built in 1848, making it the oldest on Australia's mainland. The light cast by its multiple lenses was once a beacon for every sailing ship arriving from Europe, a light of hope for the passengers and a symbol of their arrival in the New World after months of privation and illness at sea.

I climb the spiral stairs inside the lighthouse and walk out onto its balcony. The wind wraps itself around me like a straitjacket. Below me, Bass Strait is wind-driven, white-capped, livid. It is 80 kilometres from the cape across to King Island, in the centre of Bass Strait's western entrance, but such were the perils of passing through here by sailing ship that negotiating this passage was known as 'threading the needle'. Ships by the score came to grief along this coast, driven onto the rocks by gales in daylight or unable to make their way in the dark.

Is there anything quite like an old lighthouse to stir the imagination? Still buffeted by the wind, I can't tear my eyes from the raging sea that is Bass Strait, Australia's stormy portal. My grandfather's grandfather, John Lay, a 26-year-old immigrant from Wiltshire, England, would have passed through this strait on his way to Melbourne. His ship was the *Regulus*, the year was 1842 and John was accompanied by his 19-year-old bride, Emma. My great-great-grandparents, some of the immigrants who made it safely through the eye of the needle. Six years *before* this lighthouse was built.

The ocean road goes on, heading directly west. I'd seen photographs of the Twelve Apostles, but nothing quite prepared me for the sight of the real thing. They're a series of colossal rock formations standing just off the coast, in geological terms 'stacks', remnants of mainland left after wave and wind have eroded away the softer surrounding strata. Originally they were called the 'Sow and Piglets', with the largest – Muttonbird Island – the sow and the surrounding smaller surrounding islets the piglets. Later the pigs became the more decorous apostles. They're best viewed first from the foot of the Gibson Steps, near Princetown, which descend 70 metres down the cliff face to a sandy beach at its base.

Standing on the beach looking west along the irregular line of stacks, I can fully appreciate the immensity of the Twelve Apostles. Sculpted by the mighty waves rolling in from the Southern Ocean, their horizontal, multi-coloured bands of limestone strata can be matched up clearly with those of the adjacent mainland to which the stacks were once joined. Today the wind's off-shore, soothing the sea, but the waves are still huge, breaking far out and sweeping relentlessly onto the shore. What must it be like here, I wonder, when the sea is driven by a southerly gale?

I walk along the base of the cliffs, dodging the wave surges, staring upwards. The land is the colour of gingernut biscuits, and like a biscuit dunked in tea, it becomes soft, then dissolves. In this way the continent of Australia is slowly becoming smaller, at a rate of about two centimetres a year. Maybe in this part of the country, I think idly, they need to change the title of the national anthem to '*Retreat* Australia Fair'.

The drive for the next fifteen kilometres, from Princetown to Port Campbell, provides exhilarating views of the Twelve Apostles. Even better are the views from the many boardwalks and platforms placed along the tops of the cliffs, or the walking tracks winding through the heath beside them. This was a fatal shore too, known as 'the Shipwreck Coast'. More than 300 ships have been lost along here, and innumerable lives with them, victims of the violent weather, navigational error and unseen reefs.

Warrnambool is the largest settlement on the Shipwreck Coast, a town of 28,000 people. It's most notable for being a nursery for Southern Right whales, who come up from the Antarctic to give birth to their calves beside Logans Beach – just outside the town – from May through to September. Two days before I arrived a whale calved and today there's a big crowd watching her and the baby lolling about in the calm green water, only a few metres from the boogie-boarding boys zipping about in the glassy waves. A little way away another huge Southern Right – they grow up to fifteen metres long and can weigh 60 tonnes – broaches, and the crowd exclaims at the sight. How things have changed. Throughout the nineteenth century these majestic creatures were harpooned mercilessly all along this coast, hacked to bits and rendered into liquid, their bones left to litter the sands. Now they're watched, studied, revered.

I recall this welcome turnaround the following day too, when I'm being buzzed about in an inflatable among a fur seal colony on Cape Bridgewater, 60 kilometres further along the coast, near Portland. The cape is knuckle-shaped, and beside the remote rocks at the end of it dozens of fur seals are frolicking about the boat, turning corkscrew, flipping onto their backs and honking at us, then diving deep into the translucent water. They shelter on rocks in a cavern on the cape, and it's a grand sight to motor into this chamber and watch the glossy, chocolate-brown seals heaving themselves from the water, honking at one another and sliding back down the rocks like children on a hydroslide. If this were the 1800s these lovely, playful creatures too would have been mercilessly slaughtered for their skins.

'Where else are you staying on the Ocean Road?' a woman from Melbourne asks me.

After checking my itinerary I reply, 'Port Fairy', pronouncing it as it's spelt.

The woman gives me a reproachful look. 'Port *Ferry*,' she corrects me.

No self-respecting Australian would call a town after a fairy, although that's what happened in this case. The place was named after the cutter *Fairy*, by its skipper when he sailed into its sweeping bay and river mouth in 1827 in search of fresh water. Whalers and sealers followed and many pubs and trading stores were built. By the 1840s any whales in the area had all been killed, but the town survived. Today it's the prettiest place on the Shipwreck Coast, with enormously wide streets, a number of pubs dating back to the 1840s and an avenue of Norfolk pines beside the river harbour. Every March Port Fairy hosts Australia's largest folk-singing festival, and nearby Griffiths Island, at the mouth of the river, is a sanctuary for short-tailed shearwaters, commonly called muttonbirds.

With considerable regret I leave the Great Ocean Road at Portland and head inland towards South Australia. Driving through pine forests, I see lots of kangaroo carcasses beside the road, some of the carrion being pecked at by fat black crows. The 'roos, I'm told later, are the victims of the big trucks that roar along the rural roads at all hours, bowling the poor creatures right off the highway, especially at dusk and dawn.

As I get closer to the border between Victoria and South Australia I become excited, imagining that I will need to show my passport at a checkpoint, or at the very least my driver's licence. But no, there's not even a sign to mark the border between the two states. The only thing that tells me I'm now in South Australia is a notice declaring that the speed limit's 110kph, rather than Victoria's 100kph. A little later, listening to a Mt Gambier radio station, I realise I've also gained some time. Victoria's time is half an hour ahead of South Australia's.

The road – wide, and almost empty – bends westward, then after a couple of hours passes through Mount Gambier, the most diverting aspect of which is the mountain itself, an extinct volcano. There's a lake here too that changes colour, but lakes – even bi-coloured ones – seldom interest me, so I drive on through and head north-west on a road that's completely straight and flat. And it's about here that I first see the name Mary MacKillop. I'm now on, the sign tells me, the Mary MacKillop Tourist Trail. Trouble is, I've no idea who Mary MacKillop might be. Was she a nineteenth-century brothel owner, perhaps? Or a pub proprietor during the gold rush? There's nothing to inform me further, so I set the car on 110kph autopilot and head for the historic town of Penola, where I'm to stay.

'Mary MacKillop will be Australia's first saint,' I'm told by Bill Murray, a softly spoken Scot and viticulturalist, who's lived in Penola for many years. Mary was born in Fitzroy, Victoria, in 1842, the daughter of Highland Scots Catholics and the eldest of eight children. The family lived in great poverty and the children were home educated. In spite of an unhappy childhood, Mary grew into a personable and intelligent young woman, working as a governess and teacher in Penola and conscious through her own childhood of the poverty many local children were suffering. In 1861 she met a handsome, charismatic young English priest-scientist, Father Julian Woods, whose teaching inspired Mary to open a school for the children of the poor. Other young women came to join her, and in this way the Congregation of the Sisters of Saint Joseph began.

During her life Mary met with stern opposition from male church authorities. Excommunicated in 1871, she was later reinstated and continued her work for the needy. She died in Sydney in 1909, and her life of exceptional holiness was recognised with her beatification by Pope John Paul II in 1995. Once she is canonised (they need to find another miracle she wrought), Blessed Mary MacKillop will be sanctified. Already she is recognised as Australia's Mother Teresa.

There are few prettier or more historic settlements in Australia than Mary's home town, Penola. Set down on a fertile inland plain, surrounded by land as flat and brown as a poppadom, Penola lies astride the spear-straight Riddoch Highway. It's a heritage town, and proud of it. Founded as a pastoralist settlement in 1850 by Scots Catholics, it became a place where coaches, wagons and their passengers stopped over for the night on their way further inland. Today the nineteenth-century buildings which served these travellers still exist: the Cobb and Coy Booking Office (1857), the gracious old Royal Oak Hotel (1848) and Petticoat Lane, Penola's oldest street, which contains several superb examples of slab and hewn cottages, including the town's oldest house, Sharam Cottage (1850).

Mary MacKillop's humble schoolhouse is preserved in Penola, near the church and alongside the imaginatively designed and integrated Interpretive Centre, which bears her name. Built from traditional colonial materials – stone, wood and iron – but in contemporary style, the centre was opened in 1998. The building invites, then guides the visitor through displays chronicling the lives of Mary and the equally remarkable Father Julian Woods. Even for a non-believer, it is clear that something miraculous did happen in this place.

And even if the blessed Mary wasn't a tippler, she must've had no trouble obtaining wine supplies for the holy sacrament, because just a cork's pop along the road from Penola is the wine-growing district of Coonawarra, a euphonious name meaning 'honeysuckle rise' in Aboriginal. There don't seem to be any honeysuckles left here, but there are vines aplenty, hundreds upon hundreds of rows of them, occupying the level land on either side of the wide, straight Riddoch Highway.

Coonawarra has been called 'the Bordeaux of Australia'. All the country's pedigree labels are here: Penfolds, Wynns, Mildara and dozens of others less well known. Why? The answer, Bill Murray explains, lies in the soil. He shows me a metre-deep trench in a vineyard. The soil profile reveals a dark red upper layer just about a hand's width wide, and a substrata of limestone. 'The top layer's the secret,' says Bill. 'That's the *terra rosa*. And the limestone is free-draining, so the water percolates through.' I can see the roots of a vine creeping along the limestone's jointed planes. The *terra rosa* and the limestone, combined with hot dry summers and cool winters, and a high degree of oenological expertise, enable the Coonawarra to produce some of the finest cabernet sauvignon and merlot varieties in the world.

Coonawarra's *terra rosa* occupied a very limited area, a cigar-shaped district just fourteen kilometres long and about two kilometres wide. Beyond that the soil's black and less free-draining. The local joke is that the most valuable vine-growing *land lies under the main road through it*, prompting suggestions that the road be ripped up and a by-pass built around the *terra rosa*. I pace out the road and its verges. Twenty metres wide by fourteen kilometres long. Yes, that strip could produce a lot more cab sav and merlot.

◦◦◦

Driving down into the central city from the Adelaide Hills, the first impressions I register are of flatness, the width of King William Street, the city's main thoroughfare, and the right-angled avenues running off it. The city is laid out in a rigid grid. How did this urban latticework come about?

Adelaide's story begins with the visionary Colonel William Light, whose father was English and whose mother was Malay. After serving in the Royal Navy in the early years of the nineteenth century, William joined the British Army, and it was he who brought the first shipload of settlers into Gulf St Vincent, a sheltered stretch of water on the south coast of Australia, in 1836. They were mainly Scottish immigrants fleeing the domination of the Church of England, 'free' immigrants in stark contrast to the convicts being transported to settlements in New South Wales, Tasmania and Victoria.

William Light selected a site for their settlement ten kilometres from the gulf coast, on level fertile land where the bush had been burned away by local aboriginals as a hunting technique. The climate in the chosen area was a marked improvement on that of Scotland, having hot dry summers and cool to mild winters.

After the land was surveyed, the building of Adelaide began, with Light making generous provision for public parks and gardens in the town he created. It was named after the wife of King William IV of England, the only Australian capital named after a woman.

Adelaide's story is written in its avenues, parks and buildings. When I take a stroll along North Terrace, the upper west-east boundary of the city's central square mile, I find myself walking through most of South Australia's history. The boulevard is lined with stone buildings – galleries, museums and government buildings – which embody the solid success and confidence of those first Scots settlers. There's the humble original Parliament House, the neo-classical Parliament House which later replaced the first one, the Mortlock Library (where among other things, all the late great Sir Donald Bradman's cricket memorabilia is displayed), two universities, the South Australia Museum and the South Australia Art Gallery.

The gallery is magnificent, rivalling anything in Melbourne or Sydney. It accommodates the world's finest collection of Aboriginal paintings, as well as an impressive display of European and Australian paintings. Being free settlers, the founding families of South Australia were able to bring their art and furniture with them. Consequently the city inherited a wealth of antiques and paintings, many of which are on display in Adelaide's gallery. William Light was a painter too, and a self-portrait hangs on a wall of the gallery, in which he has depicted himself as a full Caucasian, rather than half Malay.

Separating Light's urban square mile and North Adelaide is Torrens Lake and a belt of open land containing the Adelaide Oval, one of the world's most picturesque cricket grounds, the zoo and Botanic Gardens. Beyond this lovely green belt is North Adelaide, which is both historic and a gourmet's heaven, crammed with restaurants, cafés and pubs. In fact everywhere I go in Adelaide I see people eating, drinking or buying food. And the whole city's such a delight to walk through that I haven't driven my car for days.

Another indelible mark that William Light made on South Australia's map was – through his role as the colony's Surveyor-General – through his decision to name the valley to the north of his city the Barossa, after the site of an English victory over the French in the Spanish Peninsula War of 1808.

For a tour of the Barossa Valley I've been provided with a chauffeur. My driver is Gavin, a podgy man of about 50. It's Saturday when we go on the tour, but Gavin is very formally dressed in a grey suit, white shirt, maroon and black striped tie and shiny dark shoes. His thinning fair hair is immaculately styled and he has a remorselessly deferential, even obsequious, manner, which puts me in mind of a funeral director. Gavin insists, in a very unAustralian way, of opening the car door for me every time we stop, then start again, treating me as if I am minor royalty. His car, a classic 1959 Chevrolet Impala, is obviously his pride and joy. Its chrome fins gleam and its shiny black paintwork and white vinyl upholstery are spotless. And as we leave Adelaide and head for the open country to the north, it becomes obvious that Gavin not only knows the Barossa intimately, he loves it ardently. And he's determined that before I leave, I'll love it too.

'You just say where you want to go, Graeme, and what you want to do, and I'll take you there.'

'Well, I haven't been there before, so you just show me the best places.'

'What a good idea, Graeme.'

We drive along quiet country lanes and through hamlets with handsome old, Bavarian-style pubs and German pastry shops. The first winemakers in the Barossa, settlers from Germany, came to the valley in the nineteenth century. Many of them anglicised their names when World War I produced an outbreak of vehement anti-German feeling. We pass the very creek of the Jacob's Creek label, where Johann Gramp first planted vines in 1847. In some of the pastures between the vineyards, grey kangaroos graze contentedly.

And over and over again, Gavin is saying, 'It's so lovely here. If only I lived in the Barossa.'

'Why don't you, then?'

'I don't know. I've always wanted to. Look at that vineyard on the hill, isn't it lovely? So peaceful. If you want me to stop anywhere, you just ask and I will. That's what I'm here for, Graeme. I want you to really enjoy yourself.'

'Thanks.'

'Now I'll show you something really interesting just up here.'

Gavin turns off the main road and along an unsealed, dusty stretch that ends at a lake that occupies a small valley. Brown grass and spindly eucalypts grow around the lake's edge, and when Gavin stops the car beside the water I see that it's not a lake but a reservoir. I also see that the still water of the reservoir is banked up behind a high, wide, curving concrete dam. From the top of the dam to the bottom it's about 80 metres, and there's a wide path along the top. Gavin rushes around to my side of the Chevrolet and opens my door.

'Now I'll show you something amazing, Graeme.'

'The dam?'

'No. Well yes, it's to do with the dam.' His face is aglow with excitement. 'It *carries sound*.'

'What do you mean?'

'If I whisper to you from the other end of the dam, you'll be able to hear me at this end.'

'Really?'

'Yes. Now you wait here, at this end, and stand beside the dam, and I'll go across to the other end.'

I'm about to tell Gavin not to bother, but already he's off, trotting along the top of the dam in his suit and heavy shoes until he's just a small figure in the distance. Then I see him scramble down beside the high, curving concrete dam face. As he does so, I put my face close to it at my end. Then I hear his excited voice, quite clearly.

'Hello Graeme. Hello. This is Gavin. Can you hear me?'

'Hello Gavin. Yes, I can hear you. Can you hear me?'

'Yes, I can. We can talk to each other, right across the dam. Isn't it fantastic?'

I almost say, 'But Gavin, we can just talk to each other like we've already been doing all day', but I don't have the heart to.

The acoustics have got something to do with the dam's curve, Gavin explains as we resume our tour. That's why it's called the Whispering Wall. And it's some time before his delight subsides, even though he must have shown visitors the trick dozens of times. Then, sighing with pleasure, he says yet again,

'It's so nice here. So peaceful, so pretty. The vineyards, the farmland. I'd love to live here.'

And again I'm thinking, *well why the hell don't you?*

We visit some wineries and I sample some of the local vintages. They're every bit as good as you'd expect. Particularly picturesque is Rockford's winery, an old stone building surrounding a cobbled courtyard. In the winery the proprietors ply me with everything from shiraz to port. Their cabernet sauvignon is my favourite. It's fruity, oaky and able-bodied, as a wine writer might say. But drinking wine and port in mid-afternoon is something I don't often do, and now I'm all Barossed out, especially after the huge lunch that Gavin insisted on buying me at another winery restaurant. So I tell him that I'd like to head back to Adelaide now.

'That's fine, Graeme. As long as you've had a good time, that's what's important to me.'

'I have, thank you.'

Still wondering, though, how anyone could be so relentlessly pleasant all the time, I ask, 'Do you do this work every day, Gavin?'

'Only at the weekends. The rest of the time I'm a funeral director.'

I fly from Adelaide to Sydney, then back to Auckland. During my time in Victoria and South Australia I've driven nearly 1500 kilometres, along the coast, through forests and farmland, city streets and suburbs, towns and villages. Gavin drove me in his car right through the Barossa Valley. My car and his car enabled me to get right up to every place I wanted to see, just when I wanted to. The only accident victims I saw were marsupials, and by not having that third lager in Apollo Bay, I avoided losing my driving licence. The car can indeed be the traveller's best friend.

But not always.

Some islands have legendary status. Think of Skye, Capri, Corfu. In the South Pacific, an ocean strewn with islands, the only one to hold this honour is Bora Bora. It's not only an island, it's a brand, spoken of in revered tones. Even the name suggests seduction. *Bor*-a, *Bor*-a.

The first sighting of the island out the plane window gives an indication of the seductive experience to come. There it is below me, a fringing reef, a bracelet of motus, an encircling lagoon whose waters are almost unbelievably variegated shades of amethyst and turquoise, and rising sheer from the lagoon a block of basalt resembling a huge impacted tooth. Two teeth, in fact, Mt Otemanu (727m) and Mt Pahia (661m), remnants of a volcano which emerged from the ocean three million years ago. Bora Bora means 'first born', as it was considered in Tahitian legend the first island to be born from the sea after its sacred neighbour, Raiatea.

The plane banks, there are glimpses of over-water bungalows wriggling out into Bora Bora's lagoon like brown caterpillars, then we are on the approach to Motu Mute ('Moo-tay'), the narrow island in the extreme north of the lagoon where the airport is located.

I seem to be the only person at the airport who's not a Japanese honeymooner. There are dozens of them, looking no older than fifteen, already with their digital cameras in action, holding Bora Bora at arm's length. The airport is unique in that all transfers take place by sea, as Motu Mute is on the outer edge of the lagoon. Bag in hand, I wait for my transfer on the big catamaran which runs a free shuttle from the airport and across the lagoon to Bora Bora's only town, Vaitape. While the honeymooners are whisked away in speedboats to their over-water bungalows, I watch from the top of the catamaran the hypnotic sight of Bora Bora's mountainous core coming closer. And as I do I can't wait to explore it. It's towering, gigantic, a monolith like nothing I've ever seen elsewhere. People sometimes think that Mt Otemanu was the Bali Hai of South Pacific fame. It isn't – the model for that island is in Vanuatu – although *Tales of the South Pacific* author James Michener did know Bora Bora, as he was stationed on the island during World War II.

During the war the American forces fully appreciated Bora Bora's unique qualities. In 1942, with the threat of an earlier, unscheduled Japanese invasion of the South Pacific, 5000 American soldiers were stationed on Bora Bora. The airstrip was built on Motu Mute, eight seven-inch artillery guns were subsequently placed around the coast and the islanders' way of life was changed forever. Fraternisation was mutually enthusiastic, though few American soldiers stayed on after the war was won to care for the children they fathered by local women. The legacy of that time is the airstrip, the gun emplacements – all but one is still in place – and an affection for Bora Bora among American celebrities which is still alive and thriving.

At my hotel, I consider the activities on offer on Bora Bora. You can feed sharks and rays, parasail, descend to the depths in a submarine, jet-ski, horse ride, indulge in a traditional Tahitian massage, take a helicopter ride, go for an excursion in a glass-bottomed boat or a catamaran. I don't want to do any of those things because they sound too dangerous – especially the massage – so I'll leave all that to the Japanese honeymooners. Instead I plan to go around the island, admire Mt Otemanu and Mt Pahia, look over the town of Vaitape and have dinner at Bloody Mary's.

The island's a bit big and my time's a bit short for me to go by my preferred means of transport, i.e. bicycle, so I decide to hire a rental car. There's an agency in Vaitape, and the girl in the office there arranges for me to have a small Renault. It's over ten years old and fairly battered, but it's all I need, so soon I'm pootling around Bora Bora's coast with no chance whatsoever of getting lost because this is virtually the only road on the island. I have to drive on the right, *a la Francais*, but it doesn't take long to adjust to this, and to changing gear with my right hand. The main problem is speed. Although the traffic's light, everyone on Bora Bora – except me – drives fast. Very fast. Very, very fast, as if they think they're competing in the Grand Prix. There are speed limit signs everywhere, 80kph on the open road and 50kph within the village districts, but the other drivers take not the slightest notice, only dropping their speed from 100kph to about 80 when they reach a village.

Are there no traffic police on the island? I wonder. Because I drive faithfully within the limits, the locals roar up behind my Renault and tailgate me fiercely, hovering just behind my car like animals of prey waiting to pounce, their headlights like great eyes, wide with aggression. And because the coast road is usually curving, the chances to safely overtake are few. So every time I'm tailgated I move far to the right on the straight stretches, letting the edgy overtakers have their way.

Most of Bora Bora's resorts are clustered around Matira Point, a beautiful spike of land to the south of the island, lined with white-sand beaches. But past Matira Point, along the eastern side of the island, it's almost unpopulated. Here there are no plantations or gardens, the coastal plain is too narrow. But the road is straighter too, meaning that the wannabe Formula 1 drivers can overtake me with ease, then vanish in seconds, so the driving becomes more relaxing.

Driving along the coast, I can see bungalows lining the beaches on a long line of motus across the shining lagoon, and speedboats zipping about, transferring more Japanese honeymooners from the airport to resort-land. But I'm more fascinated by what's to my left – the gigantic block of rock that is Mt Otemanu, soaring sheer-sided in the centre of the island. It's huge, and covered with bush, its basalt rock interior only revealed near the flat summit. The mountain is such a compelling landmark that I have to stop to photograph it. I pull onto the side of the road, turn off the engine, walk over to the other side of the road and take several shots of the mountain, suspecting that no photograph will quite do justice to its grandeur. Then I get back into the car to resume my self-drive tour. I love this, having my own car. I can go where I like, stop wherever I want to, start whenever I want to.

I turn the ignition key. Nothing. I turn it again. Nothing. Not even a flicker of current, not even a clunking sound. I wait awhile, then try again. Nothing. The battery is dead. When I look under the car's bonnet it takes me some time to find the battery and its terminals because the whole engine is encrusted with mud and dust. Hopeless. I slam the bonnet down. *Merde!* The temperature is 32 degrees Celsius, this part of the island is sparsely populated and I have no mobile phone with which to call the rental car people. I'll have to walk to the nearest house and ring from there. I raise the car's bonnet again and leave it raised, then start walking. *Useless fucking car.* Why didn't I hire a bike?

As I walk, with the massive mountain looming to my left and the silken lagoon on my right, the heat is intense. I've no idea how long I will have to walk, and I'm now very conscious of the fact that Bora Bora is inhabited by just 5757 people and about an equal number of sly, mangy, evil-looking dogs. Dogs that undoubtedly will take delight in savaging me if I trespass on their territory.

After about 20 minutes of trudging I come to a house set back a little from the road, surrounded by palm trees, on the mountain side. The front door is wide open. I glance nervously into the property. It appears to be dogless.

'Bonjour! Bonjour! Ia Orana!' I call through the open door of the house. A stout, middle-aged Tahitian woman emerges from the back of the house, bare-footed and wrapped in a red and white pareo. She does not look friendly, so I know I have to quickly convince her that my arrival on her doorstep will not be threatening.

'Ah…bonjour Madam. Pardon, mais je suis un visiteur, et ma voiture loyer c'est ….c'est …' In the heat and confusion I grope for the right word. '… ma voiture c'est *cassé*,' I gasp.

She doesn't smile, but she nods. She understands. I hand her the agreement I have signed with the rental car company, which fortunately I have brought along. The woman grunts, then goes to the back of the house, calls the rental company, returns, says in English,

'You go back to the car. You wait there. They come.'

'Merci, merci beaucoup, Madam.'

But plodding back along the road, I'm wondering how she knew I wasn't French.

'They' turn up in the form of a tubby, young gay Bora Boran who drives up to the clapped-out Renault in a near-new, silver Peugeot 307. He tries the ignition, confirms that the battery is dead and says that I can have the Peugeot instead. He will send someone to tow the Renault to a garage. Then he drives us at very high speed back to the agency office, hurtling around the bends and overtaking everything in sight, even on the bends, while I huddle in terror beside him. At the agency he hands me the new car's keys and says with an apologetic smile, 'Very sorry about the other one, M'sieur.' He ripples his fingers gaily at me. 'Bonne journée, M'sieur.'

The new car's wonderful. It's air-conditioned, there's Tahitian music on every radio station, it's automatic and I can drive as fast as the locals. In minutes the stricken Renault is forgotten. I like this car and I like this island. So much so that I drive right around Bora Bora three times.

Each time I call in to Vaitape, a dusty town spread over flat land on Bora Bora's south-west coast. It's a small passenger port with a very good waterfront craft market, a clean, well-lit supermarket, several black pearl boutiques, snack bars, banks, an internet café and other service facilities. There's also a big parking area – ideal for drivers like me who are unused to parking left-hand drive vehicles.

After my third circuit of Bora Bora I drive back to my hotel, park the car, shower and relax until the pick-up bus comes to take me to Bloody Mary's for dinner.

Bloody Mary's is just south of Vaitape, close to the lagoon. Run by two American brothers for the past 36 years, it's famous for its clientele and its menu-less cuisine. Outside the restaurant is a board that lists their eminent clients. It's a long list, and includes the likes of Janet Jackson, Gerard Depardieu, Marlon Brando, Rod Stewart, Cameron Diaz, Jimmy Buffet (he would have appreciated the buffet) and Roman Polanski. Buzz Aldrin, even.

Inside, one of the brothers, Craig, stands behind a bed of crushed ice, on which is laid out many different kinds of fish and shellfish, along with a whole mahi mahi (a tropical game fish). Craig invites the guests to order their preferences, then they are seated. The restaurant has a sand floor and tables made of polished coconut palm trunks split down the middle. There are candles on all the tables. The ceiling is draped with pale brown bamboo leaves and the whole dining area is enclosed by low walls of rounded river stones. As I sit and wait for my meal to come, a handsome ginger cat glides past my table, scratches in the sand on the floor, squats carefully and takes a piss in the crater he has made.

Cat's piss apart, Bloody Mary's is sophisticated and well run and filled with American and Japanese honeymooners. The food is good and so too is the service. When I visit the men's toilet I see that it contains an unusual feature. Dangling from a chain above the urinal is a circumcised penis made of carved, polished wood. A short sharp tug on the penis brings a flow of water into the urinal. I find myself wondering if there is any sort of equivalent feature in the ladies toilet, next door.

When I leave Bloody Mary's I present a copy of one of my books, *The Miss Tutti Frutti Contest*, to Craig, then suggest that the next time I come I might see my name too on the board outside. 'Depends what I think of the book,' he replies, not unreasonably.

The Peugeot is already parked back at my hotel. I'm very relieved that Bloody Mary's supplies free transport back to their hotels for its customers. It's a good thing; it would not have been sensible for me to get behind the wheel and drive like a local tonight. Those three vanilla rum punches I had at the restaurant have left me a little, well, punch drunk. There are times when every traveller should leave his car behind.

# The Culturally Sensitive Traveller

'Culturally sensitive'; it's an expression that has become the
traveller's bugbear. Too often it's bandied about by people who
urge an overly reverential attitude towards those whose beliefs are
different from one's own. For different, read superior. This is not
helpful, because different is *not* always better. No culture is entirely
virtuous. Our Western culture's strengths include its respect for
civil rights, general tolerance of dissent and belief in freedom
of expression; its weakness the subordination of community
responsibilities to individual self-interest. On balance, this makes
the West a much better place in which to live, which is why every
day thousands of Africans and Asians – the world's most tragic
travellers – risk their lives in leaky boats and suffocating container
lorries to get there, making a terrible mockery of their cultures'
claims to superiority over ours. There are many societies whose
cultural values are anathema to Western travellers. In China
the state executes thousands of people every year, Saudi Arabia
condones retributive amputations and beheadings, in Iran people

are stoned to death, in Mali there are brutal female circumcisions, in Australia there are endless reruns of *The Days of Our Lives*.

In the face of all this, how best can the traveller display 'cultural sensitivity'? The answer is simple; it's about using commonsense. You find out what the locals don't approve of, and you conform to this set of rules for the duration of your visit, suspending most moral judgements. When you get home you can scream blue murder about how and what they eat in Bolivia, or how they treat the dogs in Hong Kong and the cats in Cambodia, but during the time you're there, it's best to just go with the cultural flow. So people hoik on the footpath in China. Get over it. French dogs shit everywhere. Step around it. You're a vegetarian in meat-mad Argentina. Carry your own couscous.

It's important though, to be aware of what's offensive to the local population and what isn't. It's a fact that in some societies people loathe having their photograph taken, just as it's also a fact that in other societies they relish a photo opportunity. Walk through a Samoan village during the evening prayer hour in a bikini and you're likely to suffer verbal and even physical abuse. Don't complain if you can't fly out from an island in Tonga on a Sunday because in that country no planes ever fly on the Sabbath, just as you shouldn't complain if you can't find pork fillet on the menu in a kosher restaurant in Tel Aviv.

But sometimes the lessons of cultural sensitivity have to be learned the hard way.

There is a casino at the rough end of the waterfront in Papeete, the capital town of Tahiti. Like most casinos, it's garish and loud, but it does good business because a large percentage of Papeete's population is Chinese, and the Chinese have a penchant for gambling. Not having been to a real casino before, I paid it a visit. It intrigued me to see there, gathered around the roulette wheels and the blackjack tables, lines of Chinese men, their eyes locked onto the spinning wheels or the rows of cards. The light in the casino was low, the atmosphere thick with cigarette smoke. Uneven piles of coloured plastic chips on the tables indicated the success or failure of the evening's gaming. So intense were the men's expressions, so charged the atmosphere, that a photograph of the scene and a caption for it sprang into my mind. Something along the lines of *Bettors, Papeete*. I took out my Nikon, readied the flash and stood at the end of a roulette table. After the croupier spun the wheel, the concentration on the faces of the gamblers intensified. All eyes were fixed on the swirling little wheel. I raised my camera, framed the scene and pressed the shutter.

An instant after the flash went off, all eyes flicked up, and trained on me. Then hostility erupted. Two men jumped up and raised their fists, several abused me in Cantonese, one came round the table towards me, waving a forefinger angrily. I did what I always do when faced with danger – I turned and fled. And as I did, I realised (too late) that I had committed a double transgression. Firstly, the superstitious Chinese are traditionally reluctant to be photographed by strangers, because they believe the photographer is stealing their spirit. And secondly, by photographing the men in the act of gambling I was assuredly bringing bad luck down upon them, meaning that the house would clean the gamblers out. I never found out whether I was right or not in this; I was too frightened to ever go back.

But the photograph came out really well. *Bettors, Papeete. Just before they murdered me.*

The Japanese are seen in most places. They'd always seemed to me to be a tidy, tractable people who were fond of their own company. For years I'd watched them honeymooning on Bora Bora, playing golf in Queenstown, or staring out the windows of luxury coaches in cities like London and Los Angeles. I'd driven Japanese cars for years, played CDs on their stereos and DVDs on their DVD players. My fishing dinghy was powered by one of their outboard motors. Yet I had known very few Japanese people. When they travel they appear to prefer to stay in a group, guided by members of their own race. Unlike the Chinese, young and old Japanese love having their photograph taken, the young females always raising two fingers while it's done. I had observed a group of them watching a sheep-shearing demonstration on a South Island High Country farm, and it was amazing to watch their incredulous, sheep-like reactions. The Japanese seem to me to be slightly comical but at the same time somewhat unapproachable. A *Lost in Translation* race, indeed.

Yet I also know Westerners who have the greatest admiration for Japanese culture. The language, the history, the art, the ceremonies of Japan – these customs seem to take hold of Western people who have spent any time in the country. So when the opportunity came for me to travel to Japan, I did so with more than the usual curiosity. And before I went, I decided to read up about Japanese history, starting with World War II.

I had been brought up on war comics, military memoirs and novels set in South-East Asia. These invariably demonised the Japanese (only men; Japanese women didn't seem to exist) as hideous creatures who were capable of infinite cruelty to other races, bestial in their behaviour and incapable of any human feeling except a compulsion to inflict pain on their enemies, particularly Westerners. Now, as an adult, I thought these depictions must surely have been caricatures, grossly stereotypical and thus deeply offensive. To try to get things more into perspective, I began to read about the Japanese in World War II, beginning with their occupation of the Philippines.

In 1942 the Japanese Imperial Army occupied the Philippines without a shot being fired, General Douglas MacArthur having declared Manila an open city in order to save civilian lives. The

Japanese subsequently took 76,000 Filipino and Americans captive and marched them north for 120km on what became known as the Bataan Death March. Over 10,000 men died on the march, during the course of which they were given no food or water. They were kicked and beaten, and those who couldn't keep up were bayoneted.

Some of the Filipinos and Americans escaped, however, and became guerrilla soldiers, living in the hills in Manila's hinterland, harassing the Japanese whenever they could and passing on to the Allied authorities intelligence about Japanese troop movements. Although the Filipinos were Asians like the Japanese, their cultures were markedly different. Most Filipinos were Christian – strongly Roman Catholic – Western in outlook and respectful of individual rights. The Japanese attempted to gain the sympathy of the Filipinos on the basis of their shared race, but this historic example of cultural sensitivity failed utterly. Thereafter the Japanese occupation of the Philippines, like that of Burma and Singapore, was brutal and merciless. Atrocities against the civilian population were common. The hill-dwelling guerrillas were hunted down and informers used to gain information regarding their movements. Those suspected of sympathising with the guerrillas were tortured or killed.

So far, so bad. As invaders the Japanese were ruthlessly efficient; as conquerors they were brutal. This gave me pause for thought: did I really want to go to Japan, even half a century after these events occurred? Yet, I also reasoned with myself, I had travelled to Germany, and had even lived there for a while. The Germans I met had been harmless in peacetime, hospitable and, if pressed about past misdeeds, conscionable and even apologetic. Could the Japanese prove to be similarly repentant?

I read on about the war, and came across a story about which I had previously had no knowledge. It concerned the life of Father Francis Vernon Douglas, a New Zealand Catholic priest who worked in the Philippines during World War II. Written by

Patricia Brooks and published by the Missionary Society of St Columban, it told of the boy who had been born into a humble but devout Roman Catholic family in Johnsonville, Wellington, in 1910. A born leader, a talented rugby player and charismatic personality, Vernon Douglas as he was known decided to give his life to the Catholic church. He entered the seminary at Holy Cross College, Mosgiel and there trained for the priesthood. In 1937 he joined the Missionary Society of St Columban – an early Irish order – and was sent to the Philippines. Four years later the Japanese invaded and occupied the area of the Philippines where Francis Vernon Douglas lived and worked.

Father Vernon's parish was centred on the town of Paete and its large baroque stone church, which had been built in 1850 by Spanish missionaries and dedicated to St James the Apostle. Not far away, living in the mountains, were the American and Filipino resistance fighters. In July 1943, when the festival of St James was usually celebrated by the townspeople, a cordon was thrown around Paete by the Japanese military police, the Kempai-tai. Suspecting that the local population was supporting the guerrillas, those males who came to the festival from outside the town, along with the local men and boys, were detained by the Japanese military police.

The church of St James was turned into a detention centre, and those suspected of helping the guerrillas were tormented there. A method of torture favoured by the Japanese was to place the victim on the ground and pour water into his nostrils until his stomach was distended. Then a plank was laid across his stomach and two or more men jumped on it, forcing the water back up into the victim's mouth and nose, creating a drowning sensation. If the victim still failed to provide information, he was tied to the church's baptismal font and beaten with guns and swords until he talked or died. The local doctor, hoping to save the other villagers, confessed to treating sick or injured guerrillas. He was decapitated, and the torture went on.

On 24 July a tall, handsome European priest in a white soutane was brought into Paete's public square on the back of a truck. He was dragged across the square by soldiers, tied to a lamppost and left there in the heat. The 33-year-old Father Francis Douglas had been apprehended by the Japanese because he was suspected of spying for the guerrillas. In the evening he was dragged inside the church, which by now was befouled with blood and excrement. There Father Douglas was tied to the baptismal font and beaten about the head with rifle butts in an effort to make him give up information about the guerrillas. He told them nothing. He was then tied to a pillar that supported the church loft, and struck repeatedly about the face and body with bayonets for three days and nights. Still he told the Japanese nothing, although his lips moved constantly and he was observed kissing the crucifix on his rosary.

After the third day the beaten, bruised and bloodied priest was taken from the church with his hands tied behind his back and put on the tray of a truck. He was still conscious, but very weak. With the locals staring in awe at the beaten priest, Japanese soldiers pulled a sheet of canvas over his head, the truck drove away and Father Francis Vernon Douglas was never seen again. The ultimate place of death of the martyred priest remains unknown.

I put the book down, astonished by Father's Vernon's fortitude. It was a classic instance of the observation that, 'a million deaths are a statistic but a single death is a tragedy'. Other aspects of the story resonated within me. The first parish to which Father Vernon had been appointed was Opunake, the town of my Taranaki boyhood. Although my family was Protestant, I had been taught to play the piano by nuns in the local convent, beside the very church where Father Vernon had served, 25 years earlier. And I now realised the significance of the name of one of Taranaki's Catholic schools, Francis Douglas College, in New Plymouth. One of my own nephews had attended that college.

As a consequence my feelings about the Japanese turned bitter. They had tortured and killed a dedicated, decent, selfless man who had been admired by all who knew him. The contrast between the priest's nobility and his captors' monstrousness was stark. The war comics of my boyhood had been right.

So how could I possibly go to Japan now? How could I travel to a land that had treated a fellow-New Zealander and untold others with such cruelty? I would cancel my Japan trip, I decided then and there; I would go to Britain through North America instead.

But it wasn't as straightforward as that. There were other considerations, including the fact that one of my two sons, Benjamin, was living and working near Kyoto, as a co-ordinator for international relations, part of the Japan exchange and teaching programme at the community level. He had studied Japanese at school and university, was fluent in the language, and his duties involved promoting New Zealand in the community in which he lived. Now I had a problem. I wanted to see Benjamin again, but I didn't want to see Japan. Yet I couldn't do one without the other. Family loyalty won out and not long after, I flew to Osaka.

It was on the very first day in Japan that my glasses broke. The frame holding the right lens in place fell apart in my hands, leaving me one-eyed. It was hopeless, not just for general viewing of the place, but also for taking photographs. Sellotaping the lens in place didn't help because the tape obscured my vision. The frame needed soldering, or whatever the process was for repairing a broken spectacle frame. I'd been in Japan, specifically near the city of Kyoto, for less than twelve hours. It was a Sunday, and my glasses were next to useless. I was fed up.

'I'll ask Miko to help,' said Benjamin.

'Miko?'

'My supervisor at work,' he explained. He rang her, spoke in

Japanese for a few minutes, then hung up.

'Miko knows an optometrist,' Ben announced. 'She'll call him. We'll meet her at Fushimi Station at eleven o'clock.'

'Where's that?'

'About half an hour from here by train.'

Not long after I was being introduced to a petite woman, aged about 35 with a neat round face and black-rimmed glasses.

'Dad, this is Miko. Miko, this is my Dad.'

Bowing, smiling shyly, she shook my hand. Miko's car had been waiting for us at the station. We drove through very narrow, cobbled, tidy streets lined with joined apartment blocks, Ben and Miko chatting away in Japanese in the front of the car. Now the clipped, staccato cadences of the language didn't seem quite so comic to me.

The optometrist's office door opened directly onto the street, and he was waiting outside the door for us when we arrived. Miko introduced us and the optometrist, Ashiko, bowed and held out his hand. He was tall and slim, dressed in designer jeans and a white, long-sleeved shirt. Ushering us into his compact office, he held out his hand for the broken spectacles. He turned them over, looked at them closely, then said something to Miko in Japanese, before disappearing through a door. Ben translated: 'If we wait here he will fix them in his workshop at the back.'

'He works on Sundays, then,' I said to Ben.

'No, he's opened especially for us.'

We sat and waited, flicking through Japanese lifestyle magazines, depicting mainly young people leaping about in colourful clothes and clutching cuddly toys. I studied the posters on the walls of attractive young men and women, sporting fashionable glasses. All the while thinking, how much will this cost? Will my travel insurance cover it? I hadn't yet had the opportunity to get any yen. Beside me, Ben and Miko were engaged in friendly conversation, in Japanese.

After a time the optometrist returned. He handed me my

glasses, inclining his head deferentially as he did so. I looked closely at the spectacles. The right lens was firmly back in place, the frame mended invisibly. After Ashiko said something to Ben in Japanese, Ben said, 'He's also replaced …' not knowing the word in English or Japanese, he took my glasses and pointed at the two little pieces of transparent plastic attached to the inside edge of each frame, which cushion the wearer's nose '… these bits.' Sure enough, there were two new nose pads.

'Thank you, thank you very much,' I gushed. Then, nervously, I said to Ben, 'Ask him what I owe him, please.'

Ben obliged, then replied, 'There is no charge for the repair. Because you're a visitor from New Zealand, he doesn't expect to be paid.'

Further abashed, I said, 'Tell him I must pay him. For his time, at least.'

Ben spoke again, and again Ashiko made his little bowing movements. 'No,' Ben translated, 'he insists that there is nothing to pay.' And little Miko was shaking her head too, confirming there was nothing to pay.

Benjamin was living in a triangular-shaped upstairs flat, a five-minute walk from the nearest station and local shops. The flat was small, but from its miniature balcony there were views over the narrow streets below, a jumble of two and three-storeyed wooden buildings cross-hatched with power and telephone lines and topped with television antennas. On every other corner there were soft drink and snack food vending machines.

Beyond a row of tile-roofed houses was an expanse of agricultural land where young rice plants, aligned perfectly in rows, sprouted from brown watery plots. This farmland was being eaten into on all sides by construction projects: building sites for a shopping centre, an office block and apartments. Cranes, ready-mixed concrete trucks and gumbooted workers were everywhere. In the distance a range of scrub-covered hills extended across the horizon, and behind them larger cranes could be seen where the rapidly expanding town of Muko, a light industrial town, was being expanded. I leaned over the balcony rail, watching elderly women in white headscarfs bending to their work in the rice paddies.

Conga lines of navy-blue-uniformed schoolchildren were winding their way through the streets and hard-hatted construction workers were scrambling over the building sites. I heard the chimes of the electric milk delivery truck sounding. The little three-wheeled truck hove into view, then stopped at the house opposite Ben's flat. The milkman, dressed in white overalls, got out. Seeing me, he smiled, brought himself to attention and bowed.

'Good morning,' I called out.

The milkman bowed again. 'Konichi-wa,' he called out.

'Konichi-wa,' I replied.

The neighbour came out to get his milk carton, saw me, smiled, and bowed.

'Konichi-wa', 'konichi-wa', 'konichi-wa …'

Everywhere I went, everyone I met, received me with nothing but kindness. People were courteous, helpful, welcoming. The nemesis Japan I had read about seemed not to exist. It was as if World War II was a myth.

Very first impressions, though, had not been promising. Osaka, where I had left the plane, was home to eight million people, and occupied a plain, bounded on three sides by craggy hills. On a bus, looking across an elevated motorway linking Osaka with Kyoto, I saw the city sprawling away to the hills in an ugly jumble of streets, workshops, apartments, tiled roofs, neon signs, gambling halls, building sites and golf driving ranges. A network of power lines and telephone wires ran across the muddle, as if a giant, brain-damaged spider had spun a makeshift web across the cityscape. Osaka had a tangled, rickety, ramshackle appearance.

Then, looking more closely through the coach window, I saw the other Japan: patches of green shoots amongst the muddle. Bent, gumbooted women in white headscarfs, sloshed about in the paddies, tending their precious rice plants, apparently oblivious of the buildings surrounding them. Already I was finding that Japan was a juxtaposition of beauty and disfigurement, tranquillity and commotion, tradition and modernisation. But perhaps this initial impression was caused by my arrival in Osaka, second in size only to Tokyo, a port, a transport node and an industrial centre. It's the Birmingham of Japan, and who judges England by Birmingham?

Two days later, wearing my repaired glasses, I went by train with Benjamin to Nara, an inland city east of Osaka. From 710AD to 784AD, Nara was the first capital of Japan.

Nara train station stands alongside a shopping arcade which leads directly to the ancient city's heart, Yoshikien Garden and Nara Park. The garden slopes gently upwards to Mt Kasuga and its surrounding hills, and within the garden is the world's oldest wooden structure, Horyuji Temple, and the world's largest wooden structure, Todaiji Temple. Approaching the two buildings on foot along a long, wide driveway, I'm mesmerised by their scale and design. Built of dark, interlocked wood, the two temples dwarf their natural surroundings, and the people who approach and pass through them. Housed within Todaiji Temple is a colossal bronze Buddha with one hand outstretched. It too reduces us to insignificance.

Behind the temple grounds is an extension of Nara Park, where the wooded slopes and pathways are crowded with visitors and tame deer, considered divine messengers by the Japanese. The pretty, speckled animals amble about the park, waiting to be fed special biscuits that can be bought at the park's snack stalls. Wandering along the forest paths, I'm struck again by the serenity of this place. Yes, there are crowds, but they are subdued and calm – there is no loud music, no advertising hoarding, no revving vehicles – and the decorousness of the people and the scenic loveliness of the setting blends to produce an atmosphere close to complete tranquillity.

A short walk through the trees leads us to the Kasuga Taisha Shrine, noted for its rows of ancient hanging lanterns and a large 'fuji' – a wisteria vine festooned with lavender-coloured spring blooms, hanging from a wooden frame. The fuji is spectacularly beautiful, its delicate dangling blooms resembling thousands of floral ruffs. We watch dozens of Japanese people manoeuvring themselves into better low-angle positions with their cameras and camcorders, the better to capture the magnificent floral display. 'Mass wisteria,' I can't resist remarking to Ben.

Walking up a pathway through the forest, the ancient lanterns hanging from the stone wall beside us, I'm struck again by the beauty and order everywhere in this place, the complementary mixture of natural and cultural aesthetics. Yet I'm also aware that five minutes' walk away are the urban streets with their ugly confusion of overhead wires, poles and aerials, and I'm struck yet again by the paradox that is Japan: brutal war history, peace-loving present; unsightly cities, picturesque parks, teeming streets, restful reserves.

❧

'The Mayor and some of my other colleagues want us to be their guests at dinner tomorrow night,' Ben announces. 'In Kyoto.'

'Really? Why?'

'Because you're a visitor.'

'Oh.' At first I'm a bit taken aback. Then I add, 'That's very decent of them.'

Ben has already introduced me to the Mayor and some of his colleagues at the council offices where he works. Ben seems to be the only 'Gaijin' (Westerner) in the district, and as such, is a well-recognised figure. In the supermarket old ladies greet him warmly, in the railway station the ticket-seller knows him by name: 'Benjamin-san'.

His place of work is similar to any other local authority office just about anywhere in the world: cluttered desks, photocopying machines, ringing phones and people walking to and fro carrying sheets of paper in their hands. However in New Zealand offices people seldom bow to one another. Already, almost as a reflex action, I'm finding myself bowing to people to whom I'm being introduced. It's infectious, and not the kow-towing gesture I had imagined it would be. The bowing is respectful, not grovelling. Ben, thoroughly assimilated by now, even makes bowing movements when he talks on the phone. As he explains: 'The lower the bow, the deeper the respect you're showing.'

The Mayor's office, as befits his status, is spacious and orderly, and the man himself is short and balding with a bulging stomach and thin arms. He wears a beige suit, dark blue tie and thick-lensed glasses, through which he peers at me, wide-eyed, as Ben explains my work in Japanese. The Mayor, looking a little nonplussed, bows, then offers me a cigarette. Declining, I thank him for the dinner invitation. Ben translates and the Mayor nods enthusiastically. Shaking my hand, he tells Ben that he and his staff are looking forward to the occasion. Again, I'm struck by the courtesy shown towards me.

Trains, trains, trains. They have become a big part of my life; Japan is a nation that moves mainly by rail, and their trains are not only immaculate but above all, reliable. If a train from Hosono station, down the street from Ben's flat, is due to leave at 9.58am, it leaves at 9.58am. And it arrives at Kyoto when it's supposed to, exactly 73 minutes later. Railway signs are in English as well as Japanese, and the ticket machines could be operated by a 10-year old. The platforms are so clean I could eat my sushi straight off the ground, thanks to the women who patrol them day and night with their brushes and pans, vigilant in their hunt for a discarded cigarette butt or candy wrapper. The carriages are clean and comfortable, although overcrowding means it's often necessary to stand.

The place where Ben lives is a satellite town in Kyoto

Prefecture, which is right in the centre of the Kinki region; although the only kinkiness I've seen so far is in the form of an explicitly pornographic comic which the well-dressed, middle-aged man sitting next to me on the train is reading. On the way to Kyoto the train clicks its way alongside the Kizu River, passing through compact dormitory towns with chunky, grey-tiled houses and pretty, miniature gardens, then past farmland where rice shoots push insistently up through their watery beds.

The carriage gets more crowded, the buildings become denser, the farmland shrivels, the spider's web powerlines return. Then the train slips into Kyoto city (1.4 million people), the imperial capital of Japan for more than a thousand years.

Kyoto Station is a huge post-modern structure housing apartment stores, food halls and a concert stage. A series of escalators carries visitors to its roof, so partly to escape the crowds we zig-zag our way to the top from where there are 360 degree views of the city. Staring out over the mass of buildings, I see that the dense expanse of urban landscape reaches to the distant brown hills. Kyoto's sheltered, inland location gives it sweltering summers and bitterly cold winters.

Kinkakuji Temple, commonly known as the Golden Pavilion, stands on the shore of a lake, surrounded by a maple forest, in north-west Kyoto. Resplendent as it appears, the pavilion is just a replica, dating only to 1955, and since I'm in thoroughly ancient temple mode by now, this simply will not do. Moreover, the hordes of Japanese teenagers swarming and chattering on the lake paths rob the scene of much of its serenity.

More impressive and infinitely more restful is Ryoanji Temple, a 20-minute walk along the street from the Golden Pavilion. In its lake and garden setting at the foot of forested slopes, Ryoanji is a superb example of traditional Japanese architecture. Moreover, alongside the temple is a fifteenth-century 'garden' of pale, raked gravel and fifteen carefully positioned rocks. Enclosed by a stone wall, the gravel garden is about the size of a netball court. It can be contemplated in Zen-like fashion from tiered wooden steps that extend along one side of the garden. Feeling rather tired, I join other people sitting on the steps, staring silently out at the immaculately raked expanse of gravel. It's like a cream-coloured, frozen sea, swirling about the fifteen grey rocks, and its simple beauty does indeed impart feelings of serenity. After 20 minutes of staring and contemplation, I've revived enough to move on to the next temple.

On the eastern side of Kyoto is a seventeenth-century Kiyomizu temple, whose lofty pagoda soars from a hillside covered with a forest of cedar and fir. It's very impressive. And just a short bus ride away is the canal-side walk known as the Path of Philosophy, a path lined with cherry trees which leads past tea houses and small restaurants, then up a steep lane lined with little souvenir shops. At the top of the lane is Ginkakuji, also known as the Silver Temple. A raked white sand garden in the shape of Mount Fujiyama stands alongside Ginkakuji, and azalea flowers glow fluorescently amid the surrounding greenness. Again, all is beauty and tranquillity.

A wide river – at this time of year at a low level – runs through the centre of Kyoto. On one bank is an area of cafés and open-air restaurants, on the other a district of traditional, ancient housing, separated by narrow lanes, like something out of *Memoirs of a Geisha*. Here too parking space is at such a premium that outside the tiny houses small cars are stacked on top of one another with the aid of a lifting device and a metal frame. We walk across a wide bridge across the river, at one end of which is a young Scotsman in a kilt and sporran, playing a lament on the bagpipes. There is an upturned tam-o-shanter on the ground beside him. Some locals are standing around watching the piper, expressions of disbelief on their faces. Then Ben gets a ring on his mobile and, phone clapped to his ear, he is guided by the caller to the open-air restaurant where we are to be the dinner guests of the Mayor and some of his staff.

We walk through a reception area and out into a large, open-air, concreted space. Here long tables, a couple of feet off the ground and covered in white cloths, have been set. At the end of the space, down a steep concrete embankment, is the river, It's a balmy evening, and moonlight gleams on the black river water as we are shown to our places by a tiny waitress in a kimono. She bows, gestures towards one of the tables, then we sit on cushions along both sides. There are about 20 of us, men mostly, but a few women, including Miko and her husband. The Mayor is seated at the head of the table.

Porcelain carafes of sake and tiny matching cups have been set out on the table. More waitresses appear and the sake cups are filled. It's all very formal, very proper. People smile broadly at us and nod politely whenever our eyes meet. When we are all seated – Ben on my immediate right – the Mayor stands and welcomes everyone. I have no idea what he's saying, but everyone nods gravely in concurrence, including Ben. 'What did he say?' I ask Ben. 'Oh, just that he's honoured that you are here, and that he hopes you enjoy your visit.' Ben pauses. 'And that he's looking forward to hearing your speech.'

'Speech? What speech?'

'Oh yes, you're expected to make a speech.'

'You didn't tell me that.'

'I thought you'd have realised.' Ben smiles, roguishly. 'You're their guest, after all.'

I pause. 'But they won't understand what I'm saying.'

'Yes, they will. I'll translate for you.'

Ah …'

The Mayor is raising his sake cup. He calls out '*Kampai!*' and everyone replies in unison, '*Kampai!*' Then they tip their heads back and toss down the sake. I do the same. After all, when in

Kyoto, do as the Koyotes – to paraphrase that famous cliché – do. The sake has a strangely medicinal taste that is not much to my liking, but I get it down. Then Ben nudges me. 'Your turn to speak.' I get to my feet and Ben does too. Bowing in the direction of the Mayor, then to all the others – and by now this seems entirely natural – I begin my 'speech'. It's virtually all platitudes, about how welcome everyone has made us, how beautiful their city is, and how grateful and comforted my family and I are that Benjamin-san has been so well looked after in Japan.

But it's also the oddest speech I've ever made, because after each sentence I have to stop and wait for Ben to translate. It's like one of those time-delayed international interviews on TV, in which there is a noticeable gap between the question and the answer. But much more so. And as I speak, and Benjamin-san translates, the Mayor and his staff all nod constantly and murmur in what I assume is agreement. And when at last my platitude bank is close to being overdrawn and (after being prompted by Ben) I conclude with an emphatic 'Doomo arigatoo gozaimashita' ('Thank you'), there is sincere applause. Perspiring, and not just from the heat of the night, I resume my seat on the cushion and await the next round of sake. From a door to one side of the reception area, the kimono-clad waitresses are emerging, bearing the dinner on wooden platters. And more sake. And trays of bottled Kirin beer.

The food is exquisite in its presentation and bewildering in its variety. Fish, mainly, including prawn tempura sushi, grilled eel on steamed rice, flying fish roe, octopus, squid, sashimi, along with miso soup, deep-fried bean curd, teriyaki chicken, pickles, various dipping sauces and other ingredients I can't identify. There is no whale meat that I can detect. The portions are minimal, *hors d'oeuvre* size, but this doesn't matter as the dishes are being continually replenished. No one seems to mind that I'm the only one using a fork. People chat and laugh, raise their sake cups to us and toss back the rice wine. The Kirin is sipped more cautiously.

It's excellent beer though, and I much prefer it to the sake. More waitresses appear and the cups are refilled. The other guests raise their cups to Benjamin and me before they drink. Some of them begin to call out 'Cheers!' before they drink, which provokes near-hysteria. By way of reply I call out 'Kampai!', before I swallow some more Kirin. Another hysteria outbreak.

Now, at the head of the table, the Mayor is struggling to his feet. He raises his sake cup, shouts 'Chairs!' in my direction, then sits down again. Hysterical laughter all round, and echoes of 'Chairs!' 'Chairs!' 'Chairs!' from around the table.

The tiny waitresses are working very hard now, bringing more platters, more sake, more Kirin. It's all very jolly, even though I can't understand what anyone except Benjamin is saying, and even he's having trouble keeping up. And as the fevered eating and drinking goes on, I'm sober enough to realise something surprising. Almost everyone else is drunk. And getting drunker. I'd already noticed the tendency for Japanese people to become intoxicated very quickly. At a small restaurant we were at a couple of nights ago, a group of teenage girls at a neighbouring table began to shriek and dance on their table-top, after just two rounds of drinks. Their behaviour wasn't objectionable, just riotous inebriation. Geneticists have proved that some Asian races – notably the Japanese – have a gene that predisposes them to an intolerance of alcohol.

There is now ample evidence at hand that this is indeed the case. The Mayor is shouting and waving his chopsticks like the conductor of a demented orchestra. He's also gone very, very red in the face. His neck, cheeks and forehead are the colour of a boiled crayfish, and it looks to me as if he's going to explode. But he doesn't, he just goes on shouting and waving his arms about, alternately scooping up food with his chopsticks and belting back the sake. *'Chairs, chairs, chairs!'* he cries.

An hour or so later, Japanese tea is served, in bowls. I'm relieved to have some, but most of the others seem to prefer the alcohol. Now it's after ten o'clock and Benjamin and I have to catch the ten-thirty train back to Hosono station. Slowly and with great reluctance, our group gets to its feet, bows to one another, and passes out through the reception area. Matsuko-san, the council accountant, pays the bill with a credit card (I wonder if perhaps the Mayor's ratepayers are footing the bill for this), then we all traipse out onto central Kyoto's huge paved square. It's been a very, very jolly evening. In the square we shake hands and yet again there are bows all round. Ben expresses my profuse thanks to the Mayor and everyone else for the evening. 'Sayonara, sayonara,' I say over and over again. At last people trip off towards the nearest station, leaving only the Mayor and Matsuko-san with us. The Mayor's face is now the colour of a crimson camellia. He lurches forward, staggers back, then says something to Matsuko-san. They both say something to Benjamin, then together tack off across the square. 'Where are they going now?' I ask him. 'To the red light district,' Benjamin explains.

And so my experience of Japan turned out to be entirely different to what I had expected. No one showed me anything but kindness and courtesy and I felt safer in Japan than I did at most times in Auckland. Then there were those gardens and temples and parks and lakes and forests – all of which imbued me with a sense of beauty and peacefulness.

Yet I often found myself looking at the people around me, particularly while travelling on a crowded train or wandering about in a shopping arcade, disturbed by the fact that these people belonged to the same race that had tortured poor Father Francis Vernon Douglas and countless others to their deaths. In Japan I had witnessed the paradoxical scenes of side-by-side ugliness and beauty, just as the place possessed that other inherent contradiction, historical militarism and present-day concord.

A super-modern, high-speed train connects central Osaka to Kansai Airport, which has been built on an artificial island in Osaka Bay. As I wait on the platform for the next airport train to appear, I watch the station attendants and cleaners walking up and down, ensuring everything is clean and in order. Then, as the sleek train emerges from the tunnel and approaches the platform, the cleaners and attendants line up tidily and bow, deeply and respectfully to the driver. I just manage to stop myself doing likewise. And later, looking out the window of the Japan Airlines 747-400 as it backs away from the airport pier, I see the ground staff lined up, bowing to the pilot and his crew.

Flying out of Osaka and staring down at Japan's snow-topped mountains and patchwork plains, I'm still perplexed by what I've read and seen. Were the heinous events that followed Japanese expansionism in the late 1930s and early '40s just an aberration? Could it be true, as has been suggested, that *all* peoples possess the potential to persecute those racially or ideologically different to themselves, but only do so when such behaviour is fomented and sanctioned by the state? Witness Hitler's Germany, Stalin's Soviet Union, Pol Pot's Cambodia, Hutu-led Rwanda and Imperial Japan. I don't know the answer to that question. But what I do know for certain, as a result of visiting Japan, is that travel does occasionally have the capability to broaden the mind.

# The Cruising Traveller

I had never been on an ocean cruise before. I had been on cross-Channel and inter-island ferries, and once went on an overnight ferry from England to Spain, but never on a real cruise. Cruising was for old people. *Really* old people. I had watched big cruise liners tied up at city wharves mostly with feelings of pity, all those poor old people, trapped on a ship for weeks. Not able to go where they really wanted to. Being told what to do all the time. The ultimate packaged travellers. That wasn't really travelling, that wasn't for me.

Then I was offered the chance to go on a cruise through the South Pacific for a couple of weeks. The idea behind it was that I would give talks on board, about the South Pacific, and also provide readings from *The Miss Tutti Frutti Contest*, one of my travel books. I thought about it, then said 'yes'. What the hell – I now knew the cruising industry was the fastest-growing sector of the travel business; shipyards, apparently, can't keep up with the demand for building new and bigger cruise ships. It stood to reason, then, that cruising must have something going for it.

ᒐ

This is a unique view of downtown Auckland. Standing on the top deck of the P & O cruise liner *Pacific Star*, late on a mid-winter Friday afternoon, we're on a level equal to the adjacent apartments on Princes Wharf. Sailing time is now only minutes away. People in the apartments stare out at *Pacific Star*'s passengers, most of whom already have drinks in their hands. The ship's horn sounds, and we begin to slide away from the wharf and the other downtown buildings. Friends and family gathered on the wharf wave at the passengers wildly, just like they do in the old movies.

Minutes later the tug's towing lines are dropped and we're under way, gliding down the harbour with surprising speed. A light south-westerly cools the air. Yachts on their Friday afternoon races, tacking down the harbour, can't keep up with us. The afterdeck of *Pacific Star* is crowded, and neatly uniformed Asian stewardesses move among the throng, refilling glasses. The passengers' mood is ebullient, enhanced by the fact that the cloud-streaked sky over the Waitakere Ranges is taking on a beautiful blush. The deck is a moving platform five storeys high above the harbour, giving glorious views of the city in all directions. We slip past the container wharf ('Yes, I will have another glass of champagne, please') around North Head and into the Rangitoto Channel. This is the proper way to leave a port city like Auckland.

Why haven't I travelled like this before?

The first difference between this and other forms of travel becomes clear when I pack. *No weight limit.* I can take as much with me as I can carry. Not just a small bag of unsold books, but *a whole caseful*. OK, so carrying the case from the taxi to the ship is a bit of a problem; it is so heavy I strain a muscle in my back. But it's such a treat, not having to keep a weather eye on the infamous 20kg limit, the bane of all economy class air travellers.

At 35,000 tonnes *Pacific Star* is a mere sprat among cruise ships (the world's largest cruise liner, *Queen Mary 2*, which went on her maiden voyage in 2004, weighs 150,000 tonnes; some cruise ships now being built will take 3600 passengers), but *Pacific Star* can still comfortably accommodate 1400 passengers and 540 crew. Built in 1982 and refurbished in 2001, she's under the command of Captain Marco Fortezze, from Genoa, Italy. A graduate of the San Giorgio Nautical Institute, the captain makes his presence felt mainly through his twice-daily announcements from the bridge, in heavily accented English. '*Our course-a is-a north-a north-a west, our speed-a is-a sixteen-a knots.*' And at that rate it's only a couple of days before the sun becomes noticeably higher in the sky, and warmer with it. By now the ship has been thoroughly explored by the passengers, its best niches discovered. Like cats in winter, we seek out the best bits of sun, then cast ourselves down on our loungers with our eyes closed or our novels open. After a few days fundamental nautical terms – 'knots', 'aft', 'for'ard', 'mid-ship', 'port', 'starboard' – trip off our tongues unselfconsciously.

Like all modern cruise ships, *Pacific Star* is an entirely self-contained world, a floating resort, a multi-purpose, very comfortable hotel which caters to its passengers' every whim. The recreational activities are almost limitless. And how do we know what's on? We read it in the ship's newspaper.

*Pacific Daily* appears magically in our cabins every evening and quickly becomes indispensable. Its four pages tell us everything we need to know about each day at sea: dining hours, daily activities and entertainment, as well as background information about the islands we call at. Mostly though, it details shipboard activities. On a typical day on *Pacific Star* you can: join an earring-making class, bid for a painting at the art auction, play roulette or blackjack in the casino, have a facial in the Lotus Spa, take part in a trivia quiz, paint your own T-shirt, play bingo, do line dancing, learn ballroom dancing, get taught quilting or cross-stitch, have your teeth whitened, attend a culinary demonstration, watch a movie, play table tennis/deck quoits/shuffleboard/golf putting, work out on the gym's treadmill, shop in the boutiques or sweat in the sauna. There are Internet facilities on board and big screens in the Casablanca Lounge, where we can follow global sports events live. Aussie Rules from Melbourne, rugby from Wellington.

And whichever way you choose to pass the day, you're always within sight of the dark blue ocean, and the steadily heaving horizon. The ship's stabilisers keep *Pacific Star* on a remarkably even keel, even when the winds begin to gust to 40 knots. In every direction is the ocean, apparently limitless. No land, no other vessels. The indigo water is flecked with white, but the ship cleaves the swells effortlessly, the flecks on the sea's surface appearing as bursts of white, which then slowly dissolve into the blue. There is an illusion that the ocean is streaming past the ship, as if we are still and the ocean is racing away on either side of us, like a wide river in spate. For someone who loves the sea as much as I do, this is a total immersion course.

I keep a log. An entry reads:

*SUNDAY, 11 JUNE*

**25° south latitude, 173° east longitude. Ship's speed 10.5 knots, course north/north-west. Sea 'moderate'. 710 nautical miles since Auckland. Clear skies, temperature 22°C.**

**A very strong northerly wind, gusting heavily. The sea is very lumpy. Hard to find a sheltered place on deck, but eventually I do, on the 'Oasis', the very top deck. Here by late morning the sun is strong and very welcome. But the wind makes the going difficult. At one stage it blew the coffee right out of my polystyrene cup and down the front of my trousers. From the masthead the ship's flag is flapping noisily.**

An item in *Pacific Daily* says, 'Nine-thirty this morning, Pacific Lounge. Author Graeme Lay will give a talk on the subject of the South Pacific'. Now I'm apprehensive about this. How can I compete with earring-making, cross-stitch or the art auction, all of which are on at the same time? And the Pacific Lounge is huge; it can seat the entire ship's complement. A small audience will look very small indeed. I take my notes and a pile of unsold books into the lounge at nine-fifteen, climb up onto the stage and wait. At twenty-five past nine, two old ladies come tottering down the aisle, collapse into the front row and stare up at me with what looks like confusion. Three minutes later, another pair of ladies appears, then a group of five, then a family of four. By nine-thirty there are about 30 people in the lounge, occupying only a fraction of the available seats. But they're an attentive audience and afterwards ask questions which showed that they must really have been listening.

At the end of the talk one elderly woman approaches and says, 'I only came because I thought it was cross-stitch. But I quite enjoyed it all the same.' Several people want to buy my books, but now I have a problem. The ship is cashless, everything bought is paid for by a 'cruise card'. But they can't pay for my books with the cruise card, my enterprise is completely independent of the ship's other merchandising. So the book-buyers have to produce whatever cash they have, in various currencies – Aussie dollars, American dollars, Euros – so that not only do I have to provide change or credit, I have to become a bureau de change as well. It's messy, and for days afterwards old ladies try to push stray notes under my cabin door or stop me in the dining room and thrust handfuls of Australian coins into mine. But I enjoy giving the on-board talks, speaking about islands located in the very ocean that's sliding past the portholes of the Pacific Lounge, and the people who inhabit them.

Studying a map of the ship's course, which is updated daily and posted on a noticeboard near the Lido deck of *Pacific Star*, a place-name catches my attention. We are nearing a stretch of sea named Bligh Water. That sends me scurrying to my cabin for a book on the *Bounty* mutiny.

*'Therefore, after examining our stock of provisions … we bore away across the sea, where the navigation is but little known and in a small boat twenty-three feet long from stem to stern, deep loaded with eighteen men; without a chart, and nothing but my own recollection and general knowledge of the situation of places, assisted by a book of longitudes and latitudes to guide us.'*

This was a cruise of a very different kind. The writer was William Bligh, the date 3 May 1789. After being dispossessed of the captaincy of his ship, *Bounty*, by his second-in-command Fletcher Christian, Bligh and the eighteen men who had remained loyal to him were cast adrift in the ship's skiff, off the island of Tofua, in central Tonga. They could not sail back to Tahiti, where they had been encamped for months collecting young breadfruit trees, because the trade winds would be against them. To make for Tongatapu, the main island of Tonga, was too risky – already one of the loyal seamen, John Norton, had been killed on Tofua – so Bligh decided to set sail for the established Dutch settlement of Timor, '1,200 leagues' (6000km) away to the north west

The odds against the voyage succeeding were formidable. Conditions on the skiff were so crowded that no one could lie down to rest. There was so little freeboard that it was necessary to bail constantly. Food supplies were limited to ship's biscuits, salt pork, rum (five quarts), wine (three bottles), water (28 gallons), a few coconuts and some breadfruit. Punctilious organiser that he was, Bligh allotted daily rations, weighing the food in scales fashioned from a pair of coconut shells and using a pistol ball for a weight.

In Bligh's favour was his South Seas experience – his 'own recollection'. He had been master on *Resolution* on James Cook's third voyage, so had been with Cook when the 1774 expedition briefly touched the islands towards which they were now heading. Bligh was also a consummate navigator. But he well remembered too something else he had learned fifteen years earlier. The inhabitants of the islands that lay just ahead, the Tongans had told Bligh, were dreaded for their ferocity and their love of cooking and eating the body parts of their enemies, sometimes while they were still alive. They knew the islands as 'Fidgee'. Bligh and his men had no option but to sail right through these 'Cannibal Isles' at the early stage of their long voyage to Timor.

Today I'm a guest on the bridge of *Pacific Star*. The ship is cruising at 18 knots, pitching regularly as she cuts through the ocean swells. Our course is south-west as we make for the Yasawa Islands of Fiji. Amid the array of panels, dials and radar screens extending across the ship's bridge is a large chart of this part of the Fiji Islands. Now I can study the details of Bligh Water, an expanse of sea between the Yasawa group and the northern coast of Fiji's largest island, Viti Levu. It's strewn with coral reefs, islets and shoals. Perilous waters, in more than one respect.

From 5–6 May 1789, William Bligh and his men sailed past the Lau Group of 'Fidgee', then sighted Gau, Batiki, Koro, Wakaya and Ovalau to the east of Viti Levu. Bligh charted the position of every island they saw. Then they passed through the Vatu-I-Ra channel, between Viti Levu and Vanua Levu, Fiji's second-largest island, and entered the waters east of the Yasawas.

Consulting *Pacific Star*'s charts again, I see that the Yasawas are an archipelago of extinct volcanic islands, extending in an almost straight line for 90 kilometres. The islands are steep-sided, and the reefs and shoals surrounding them like a minefield mean that *Pacific Star* must stay well away from their shores. As the Master guides the ship towards the northernmost island, Yasawa-I-Rara, the wind is gusting to 40 knots and the sea is strewn with white caps. *Pacific Star* is rolling now, and her outer decks are drenched with spray. But through the sea mist I can now see the long, grey-blue profile of Yasawa-I-Rara island.

In their overladen skiff, Bligh and his men approached the Yasawa Islands, seeking a way through them to the open sea beyond. It must have maddened the Englishmen to observe the fresh water streams that poured down the islands' sides, and the lush crops of yams and bananas on the coast, when they were surviving on a daily intake of a mere 'half gill' (an eighth of a pint) of stale water and two ounces of mouldy bread. And as Bligh and his men were unarmed, their situation was doubly perilous. They knew that from the islands' vantage points, look-outs would be watching for foreign craft such as theirs, and if taken by the locals they would be, in the words of one chronicler of Fijian custom, 'doomed by the ancient law to the bamboo knives, the heated stone ovens and the cannibal maw'.

On 7 May the Englishmen's worst fears were realised. As they passed the island of Waya, two large sailing canoes put out to sea and began to pursue the skiff. Bligh managed to sail the boat through a passage in the reef, but as he did so the wind dropped away. Immediately he ordered six men to take to the oars. The boat put on speed, bearing away to the north-west, but the canoes continued the chase. For three hours Bligh urged his men to dig ever deeper with the oars, but the Fijians' canoes were faster and began to close steadily on them. Then a stroke of good fortune occurred; a squall swept across the sea, and black clouds and driving rain made visibility poor. When the sky cleared only one canoe could now be seen, but it was still giving chase. However the wind returned and the skiff's mainsail was raised, enabling Bligh and his crew to keep their distance, and at sunset the Fijians' canoe turned back towards the island, while the skiff headed out into the open sea. But although the Englishmen had escaped 'the cannibal maw', they still had to cross well over 5000 km of open ocean.

While *Pacific Star*'s anchors hold her fast in the bay, the passengers are tendered ashore to Yasawa-I-Rara. On this lovely island I scale a basalt promontory to survey the terrain. The island is shaped like a metal staple, its narrow middle lined on the west by beaches of golden sand and on the eastern coast by rocks, reefs and wind-driven seas. *Bligh Water*. As I'm standing atop the promontory, buffeted by the wind, with little warning the sky darkens to a graphite shade, the wind grows even stronger and a squall sweeps down from the sky and across the island, drenching everything, tearing at the palm trees and lashing the waters of the bay.

Half an hour later the sky is clear again and Yasawa-I-Rara is bathed in sunshine. And I think of Bligh and his men, for whom such a squall was a godsend. And not just for concealment from the pursuing Fijians. By collecting some of the rainfall the Englishmen obtained drinking water which enabled them to survive the next stage of their long voyage. And in spite of the appalling conditions, Bligh maintained his log diligently. He wrote:

> '*Being constantly wet it is with the utmost difficulty I can open a book to write, and I am sensible that I can do no more than point out where these lands are to be found, and to give an idea of their extent.*'

Yet he managed to be the first person to record no fewer than 23 of the islands of Fiji, and even today the chart he drew comprises a reliable guide to anyone sailing through Bligh Water.

It is one of anthropology's great ironies that the people of Fiji are now renowned for their hospitality and spontaneous goodwill. On Yasawa-I-Rara the local villagers have set up their craft stalls under the palm trees. Everyone beams and greets me warmly – 'Bula', 'Bula', 'Vinaka', 'Vinaka' – even as they offer for sale replica carved cannibal clubs and the long-tined wooden forks that were used to eat human flesh. Some of the male passengers from *Pacific Star* are invited to take part in a kava session, under a canvas canopy beneath the coconut palms. All day long the Fijian men and their guests sit there, cross-legged, playing the guitar and drinking kava in the traditional way, accompanied by a clap of the hands and grunts of satisfaction.

Back on *Pacific Star* I chat with the ship's navigator, Graziano Napolitano, from Sicily. He shows me the course he has set from Yasawa-I-Rara to Suva, on Viti Levu's south coast. Graziano's course will take us to the south of the big island and through the Kandavu Passage. Bligh's course between Viti Levu and Vanua Levu would be much too hazardous for *Pacific Star*, the navigator explains. The currents are too strong, the waters too shallow, the reefs too close. For environmental as well as safety reasons, today's ships must, by international maritime law, keep a minimum of four miles from coral reefs, discharging as they do both 'black' and 'grey' waste water, from a ship's toilets and laundries respectively.

Graziano the navigator also tells me that although today electronic charts can be immediately updated, to incorporate changes like new lights or recent wrecks, he still prefers to set his courses from paper charts. To rely on electronic navigation is too risky, he maintains. He also laments the fact that today's junior officers are not taught the traditional skills of seamanship at nautical school, the time-honoured skills of celestial navigation and sextant use, which he – at the grand old age of 35 – still loves to put into practice. It's my guess that Graziano would have greatly admired the navigation skills of William Bligh, had he been among his crew.

The following day, with *Pacific Star* tied up beside Kings Wharf in central Suva, I visit the excellent Fiji Museum. Among the exhibits is the rudder from Bligh's *Bounty*, salvaged from the ill-fated ship after it was scuttled off Pitcairn Island in 1790 by Fletcher Christian and the other mutineers. Worm-riddled and grey with age, the rudder is still encased in its iron brackets, and resembles an antique plough. And as I stare at the relic, all the stories of the mutiny and the struggle of the men against the sea come flooding back. Bligh made it to Timor without the loss of a single man, landing at Kupang on 14 June 1789, after 41 days at sea, one of the most heroic feats of navigation and survival in maritime history. From Timor, Bligh returned to England, where he was absolved of blame for the mutiny. The Royal Navy then instigated a relentless pursuit of the mutineers throughout the South Pacific, led by the navy's most callous commander, Captain Edward Edwards, in the frigate *Pandora*. He clapped in irons even the Bligh loyalists who had been returned to Tahiti by Christian, taking them in an iron cage ('Pandora's Box') back to England. Three mutineers – Ellison, Burkett and Millward – were hanged publicly on the deck of HMS *Brunswick*, on 29 October 1792. Fletcher Christian and his followers, by now on Pitcairn Island, were however never found by the navy. The rest is history. Hollywood history.

*Pacific Star*'s refitted cabins (sorry, 'staterooms') are extremely comfortable. A two-berth outside stateroom features a queen-sized bed, a spacious wardrobe, an ensuite bathroom and shower, a TV and a large window. The room is air-conditioned and serviced daily. Then there are the meals. For many passengers, eating seems to be a constant pastime. And this is understandable, as all meals are included in the cruise price. But it's still surprising how much some people can eat, especially the elderly. One very skinny man in his eighties is eating every time I see him, sitting at the same table on the afterdeck, hoeing into a plate heaped with everything the buffet has to offer, then returning for more. Cruising to eat.

Breakfast, lunch, afternoon teas and dinners are prepared in the galley under the supervision of Executive Chef Eduardo Ramos and served under the watchful eye of his namesake, Maitre d'hotel, Eduardo Manuel Ramos. The logistics of the daily preparation and supply of meals to nearly 2000 passengers and crew are mind-blowing. A 10-day cruise will typically consume 1625kg beef, 1087kg bacon, 2500kg rice, 5000 litres milk, 2812kg chicken, 3750 dozen eggs, 200 cases of wine and 900 cases of beer.

 

It's often assumed that cruising is for the nearly dead. Certainly, the aged are well represented on board. For them a cruise is thoroughly safe and secure. They are seen around the ship, often with sticks and walking frames, hobbling gamely along the corridors to and from the restaurants and snatching at the rails in rough seas. But *Pacific Star*'s passengers are also drawn from the younger ranks. There are many parents with young children – the ship provides full child-care facilities, overseen by qualified teachers – as well as loads of middle-aged couples. Mercifully, there are few teenagers, but the few on board are provided with their own gathering place, the Teen Centre, where they are free to be horrid only to each other.

Moving on a steady north-west course, *Pacific Star* enters Vanuatuan waters.

 

On 16 July 1774, on his second voyage of Pacific exploration, Captain James Cook sailed into an archipelago which had been partly chartered by his French counterpart, Louise-Antoine de Bougainville six years earlier. Bougainville had named the islands Les Grandes Cyclades, after an island in Greece. However the islands' softly contoured, forested hills reminded James Cook strongly of the western Scottish Isles, and so he named them, 'The New Hebrides'. The very first European to come across the archipelago had been Pedro Fernandez de Quiros, a Portuguese heading a Spanish expedition out of South America. He and his two ships sailed into Big Bay, in northern Espiritu Santo, in May

1606. Being a devout Catholic, Quiros named the island Espiritu Santo, meaning 'Southern Land of the Holy Spirit'.

For 74 years – from 1906 until 1980 – the islands were jointly ruled by Britain and France, two countries not renowned for ever running anything together happily, let alone a whole country. This system was known as a 'condominium', and it entailed a costly duplication of all services and both languages. It's said that every morning a man armed with a spirit level scaled the two flagpoles bearing the Union Jack and the Tricoleurs, to ensure that the two flags were flying at exactly the same height. And the name New Hebrides endured until the islands achieved self-government in 1980. Since then they have been called 'Vanuatu', which means 'Our Land'.

Vanuatu comprises 70 islands – 12 major and 58 much smaller ones – and all are of volcanic origin. Located astride a zone where two gigantic tectonic plates come together, several of Vanuatu's islands are highly eruptive, notably Tanna Island in the south, Ambrym in the central zone and Banks Islands in the north. Scattered over a north-south axis from 13° to 20° south of the equator, the islands are home to 200,000 indigenous Melanesian people, called 'Ni-Vanuatu'. These people speak over 100 distinct languages, necessitating the use of a *lingua franca*, Bislama, or 'pidgin English'.

*13 JUNE. LAMEN BAY, EPI ISLAND*

Now I understand why James Cook named Vanuatu after the New Hebrides. Pacific Star is gliding past this long island, and its contours are indeed soft and gently rounded. There are none of the jagged peaks of Rarotonga or Tahiti here, at least not in the central zone of Vanuatu. Epi Island is long and undulating, its hills completely covered with coconut palms. The ship anchors in Lamen Bay, an expanse of water sheltered by Epi's hills and Lamen Island, a few kilometres from the main island. Pacific Daily has informed us that Lamen Bay is home to the gentle dugong, the so-called 'sea cow', an herbivorous mammal and an endangered species. In particular there's a large male dugong, we're told, which frequents the bay and allows people to snorkel alongside him, and I'm excited by this prospect.

Whenever *Pacific Star* anchors off-shore, a huge banner is tied to the side of the ship, stating unequivocally KEEP FIFTY METRES AWAY. Cruise ships have been a target for pirates and fanatical Islamists off the coast of Africa and the Mediterranean, and even in these placid waters no one's taking any chances. Although I wonder – each time I see the banner hung out – just what firepower is available to the crew should a violation of the 50-metre rule occur.

We're shuttled ashore on the ship's tenders and invade Lamen Bay. There's a long sweep of black sand beach ending at an airstrip, and a coastal plain covered in coconut palms, chestnut and acacia trees, backed by wooded hills. The village is strung out along an unsealed road that lines the foreshore, passing a score of thatched bures. The village people – to whom we must seem the usual mixture of ludicrousness and economic possibilities – are waiting under the palms with their wares: turtle and dugong carvings, shell necklaces, barbed spears, sarongs, brown-skinned dolls and various fruits. They only get three or four cruise ships a year calling here, so the locals have to get as much as they can from the occasion. Mostly the stalls under the trees are 'manned' by women, all clad in bright mission dresses. The one village shop sells canned soft drinks, chocolate biscuits and, absurdly on an island surrounded by fishing grounds, canned mackerel.

The Vanuatuan people are lovely – shy and undemonstrative. There's no pestering to buy goods, and the most popular attraction on the shore of Lamen Bay on this particular occasion is a children's choir who are fund-raising by singing hymns, accompanied by a group of adults playing guitars. Their sweet harmonies and shy smiles are irresistible, and there are few people who don't drop money in their bucket. After walking from one end of the village to the other, I don mask and snorkel and enter the water in search of the friendly dugong. I see plenty of small fish, but the only creatures resembling a dugong are the fat white passengers from *Pacific Star*, floundering about in the shallows. The amiable male dugong has evidently beat it for the day, and that's understandable, given the invasion of his habitat.

There is a road which strikes inland from the village, and I walk along it for 15 minutes, passing among other buildings a plain Presbyterian church lined with wide verandas on both sides, then a neat, modern primary school. I ask a man carrying a bunch of bananas how long it takes to walk across the island. 'One … hour,' he replies carefully, and I turn back. I wouldn't want to get stranded on Epi Island. It's lovely – tranquil, unhurried, hospitable – but what would you do here? And what do the local children do after they've finished their schooling? Do they get sent to Port Vila for tertiary studies? If so, then what? This is an age-old South Pacific dilemma.

On the way back to the wharf I'm stopped by a European woman with long brown hair and an earnest expression. In her mid-20s, she's a Peace Corps worker from Atlanta, Georgia, and she's teaching primary children in the village. She asks me if her pupils can practise their English with me. Of course. The children are painfully shy, but they have their questions carefully prepared. 'What is your name?' 'Where are you from?' 'What is your work?' They are very sweet, and again I think, as long as they're content to stay on this island, then that's okay. But what if they have further aspirations …?

At sunset we sail away, like aliens from another cosmos, leaving the Epi Islanders to their hymn-singing, fund-raising and dugong carving.

Mooring lines are dropped and *Pacific Star* is tethered to the wharf at Luganville, the main town of Espiritu Santo. An excursion to a neighbouring island is cancelled because of the wind. A visit upriver in a dugout canoe in the rain to a village does not appeal, so there's nothing else to do except pay Luganville a visit. Most of the other passengers are doing the same, setting out on foot along the wharf to the road that leads to the town.

First though, we have to pass a long line of local people who have set up the ubiquitous craft and souvenir stalls on the side of the road. Although the rain is light, it's persistent, and the wind is gusting straight down the coast. The stall-holders – again, mostly women – have put plastic sheets over their stalls, but the wind is playing havoc with these attempts at shelter. Few people are stopping to buy; they're keen to get on into the town, to the proper shops. The rain gets in around the stall-holders' plastic sheets and dampens their carvings, textiles and shell jewellery. The sarongs are sodden and the wind is wrapping them around each other. It's one of the saddest sights I've seen.

All along the side of the road the locals are doing their very best in the inclement conditions. A little girl in a saturated mission dress is trying to sell two tiny turtles in a bucket, another one is offering to have her photo taken with two colourful parrots perched on a string; another tiny girl is dressed in 'kastom' clothing, her stern, cannibal-costumed father sitting on a plastic chair behind her. But there aren't many takers, it's too wet for photographs. There's interest in the old Coca Cola bottles, the shapely, pale green glass ones from the 1930s and '40s. There are quite a few of them for sale, for a few dollars each. The answer to how these antique coke bottles come to be here lies in the war.

During World War II, the islands then called the New Hebrides lay in the path of Japanese forces advancing from the north. As the largest island of the strategically vital New Hebrides, and with its sheltered harbour on the south-east coast, post-Pearl Harbour Espiritu Santo was designated a key military staging post for the Coral Sea battles by the American authorities. From May to July 1942 over 100,000 Americans arrived on the island, transforming it into a military complex, complete with wharves, roads, bridges, cinemas, hospitals and airfields. Distinctively rounded, corrugated iron buildings called Quonset huts were built on the island. Among the American servicemen stationed on Espiritu Santo was James Michener, the writer who later won fame as author of *Tales of the South Pacific*. The magical island of Bali Hai, which features in *Tales* and memorably in the classic movie *South Pacific*, was modelled on the rugged island of Ambae, to the east of Espiritu Santo.

When the war ended in 1945 Espiritu Santo became a huge dump for the now-unwanted war matériel. The Americans offered the war surplus for purchase to local planters and the condominium government, but even when the price offered fell to eight cents in the dollar, the deal fell through. Rather than give it away, the Americans then decided to tip everything into the sea, at a point on the south-eastern extremity of the island. Into the sea went trucks, jeeps, planes, earth-moving equipment, canned food and crates of Coca Cola. Today the place is known as Million Dollar Point, and it's popular with snorkellers who can swim among the coral-encrusted World War II junk. Hence those emblematic 1940s American art trouveau objects for sale in Luganville this morning, dozens of Coca Cola bottles, salvaged from Million Dollar Point.

Another relic of the war is today Espiritu Santo's principal tourist attraction, in the form of the underwater wreck of the 22,000 tonne SS *President Coolidge*, which sank after striking two 'friendly' American mines in Segond Channel just east of

Luganville, in October 1942. The ship was a 1930s luxury liner that had been converted to a troop carrier, and was carrying 5000 men when it sank. All but two of the troops reached the safety of the shore. Two hundred and two metres long, the *President Coolidge* is the world's largest, most accessible wreck dive site. But the dive should only be attempted, I read, with scuba gear and an experienced guide, so that rules it out for me as a way of spending the day ashore in Luganville. I'm a snorkeller, not a scuba diver, but many on *Pacific Star* are real divers, and they're bussed off happily from the wharf to explore the wreck.

Meanwhile, the rest of us trudge along the road and into Luganville, which is strung out along Boulevard Higginson, an Anglo-French name presumably inherited from condominium days. It was here in 1980, two months before Vanuatu achieved independence, that a local man called Jimmy Stevens attempted to stage a coup d'etat and take over Luganville and Espiritu Santo. Armed mainly with bows and arrows, Stevens and his followers, known as the Nagriamel Movement, occupied the town, looted its shops and proclaimed the island's independence, calling the newly born nation Vemarana. It lasted only three months. The central government of Vanuatu brought in soldiers from Papua New Guinea who restored order and arrested the secessionist ringleaders, including Jimmy Stevens.

Along the road to Luganville there are many battered taxis with importuning drivers, large 4WDs which splash through the pot-holes, and women pedestrians in colourful mission dresses. They all greet us with shy smiles. We continue up the straggling street in the light rain, calling in for a look over the stores that sell everything from Brazilian machetes to Thai tinned tuna to Chinese cargo pants. Seeking evidence of French influence here, I find it only in the street names: Boulevard du General de Gaulle, Rue Paul Gauguin, Rue La Perouse.

We come to the municipal offices, which appear to be suffering severely from deferred maintenance. Many men are hanging about the entrance, not all of them young. Someone tells me later that the unemployment rate on the island is 70 percent, aggravated by the recent closure of an abattoir and a dive school. Maybe the island would be more aptly named 'Dispiritu Santo'. Next door to the municipal office is the town's covered market, where the main products for sale are jumbo-sized root crops, but it's a gloomy and listless place. Now that we've seen the town, there's little else to do except return to the ship.

Back on board, though, the scuba divers among us exclaim at their experience of exploring the SS *President Coolidge*. 'It's like diving right into the 1930s and the 1940s,' one diver tells me. 'There are relics of its luxury liner days as well as all the war stuff.' He and the others wear T-shirts proclaiming 'I dived the SS *President Coolidge*', so at least the shirt-sellers have done well out of the day.

The staff of *Pacific Star* are mostly in their twenties, and come mainly from the Philippines, Indonesia, Thailand and India. These young men and women are one of the delights of the cruise. They're unfailingly civil, immaculately groomed and thoroughly obliging. Nothing is too much trouble for them, yet at the same time there is none of the servility which sometimes accompanies Asian staff. Our waiter at evening meals, Sam, comes from west Java. The father of four, he is at sea for ten months, then returns home for two months' leave. Sam is attentive and considerate, with a winning smile. The crew is not only multi-racial, it's multi-national as well: Italian Master, Scottish Chief Engineer, English Chief Purser, Indian Assistant Pursers and so on. Then one morning, coming out of my cabin, I see a group of European men fiddling with a heap of flex cascading out of an opening in the ceiling. They're speaking a strange language. Curiosity aroused, I say to one of them, 'Excuse me, but where are you blokes from?' Turning towards me, he frowns and replies tersely, 'Poland.' Another example of Poland's greatest twenty-first century export: electricians.

**Off Pentecost Island, 16° south latitude, 168° east latitude. Winds averaging 30 knots gusting to 40. At 0900 there is an announcement from Captain Fortezze.**

'Ladies and-a gentlemen, after two attempts to anchor here-a, I have-a made the decision not to stop-a here-a at Pentecost Island. Passenger safety being my main-a consideration, it would-a not be safe enough-a to do so. Con-sequen-telly, we will-a instead make-a a course for Port-a Vila.'

Through the porthole I can see Pentecost, the island where bungee jumping was invented, and where, presumably, the jumpers are waiting for us, poised on their platforms. Through the mist I can see that the island is forested, its spine covered in cloud. But the sea is too rough, the swells too steep, and the Pentecostal jumpers will have to wait for another day and another cruise ship, before they once more launch themselves into space for the tourists.

*SATURDAY, 17 JUNE, 1700 HOURS.*
*Pacific Star* **is nudged by a tug up to the wharf at Port Vila.**

A cruise ship's arrival and departure schedule is carefully planned. Arrivals are timed for evening or early morning, departures late afternoon or early evening. This gives passengers an entire day in port, and on-shore excursions are heavily promoted. During the

24 hours *Pacific Star* is tied up at the wharf in Port Vila, I read in *Pacific Daily* that it's possible for me to go on a tour around Efate, snorkel in the lagoon, or visit a Ni-Vanuatu village and experience traditional 'kastom'. I decide to pass on these organised activities and instead explore the town of Port Vila on foot.

After passing through the ship's rigorous security system, which involved a passport and cruise card check as well as having all my hand luggage x-rayed to ensure, among other things, that I was not carrying any food, I walk out onto the wharf. There the locals have set up dozens of craft and souvenir stalls, selling the now-familiar objects: plastic garlands, shell earrings, wooden spears, tropical shirts, straw hats, back-scratchers and beer glass insulators with 'Bia Blong Mi' ('My Beer') written on them. A six-piece male band in gaily patterned blue-green shirts is playing reggae-type music with guitars, ukeleles and a large drum. And thankfully, it's not raining here, so the musicians and stall-holders are doing better business than the hapless ones on Luganville wharf.

Port Vila was declared a tax haven in 1970 and two years later a substantial wharf at the southern end of the town was built. Today up to 40 cruise ships a year make the capital a port-of-call, while most of Vanuatu's leading holiday resorts are located in or around Port Vila. The town has a lovely setting, scattered around a sweep of bay and up a range of sheltering hills. Ironwood trees line the waterfront and spreading acacia trees overlook the town. Sheltering Port Vila from the sea is a hilly, forested island just off-shore, called Iririki. Many international cruising yachts make anchorage between Iririki and the main island, while visitors can pop over to the attractive inshore island on a free shuttleboat to enjoy its harbour views and forest walks.

Port Vila's long main street is set just back from a grassy reserve along the waterfront. It's a treat to be in a real town again, with proper shops and supermarkets and banks and ATMs and cafés and restaurants. The main street is crowded too, with vehicles and pedestrians. The only problem is the lack of pedestrian crossings on the one-way street, Lini Highway. It's a case of pause, look, then sprint to get from one side of the street to the other.

The waterfront reserve is the location for a number of colourful craft stalls as well as a venue for outdoor rallies. Today there's a rally, led by women, which seems to be on the subject of family violence. I stop and watch the speeches being made from a stage, but can't understand much. But although the subject may be violence, the speech-makers all seem very relaxed and good-natured about it. Even the few men watching don't show any twitchiness. And here, at last, I find a sign that Vanuatu is indeed half-French – a group of local men playing petanque on a strip of dry ground at one end of the reserve. The men make their tosses, then stand about thoughtfully, hands clasped behind their backs in lengthy contemplation of the juxtaposition of their balls.

Near the centre is the town's produce market, an extensive, open-sided place of sale for fruit and vegetables. It's a good place in which to wander and see not only the range of fruit and vegetables for sale, but also to wonder at their gargantuan proportions. Everything here seems outsized: giant yams, bunches of huge bananas, enormous pawpaws, mountains of coconuts and grapefruit the size of medicine balls. Many foods must still be cooked here in earth ovens, because cords of firewood are also on sale in the market. By mid-morning the earth ovens' contents are being unwrapped, the banana leaves peeled back by women to reveal succulent chunks of chicken, beef and fish. At the rear of the market you can partake of this and other local foods, including Vanuatu's national dish, laplap, a paste made of manioc, taro or yams, to which coconut cream and pieces of pork, fish, chicken or fish have been added.

When travelling, I've found that you can learn quite a lot about a country by paying close attention to reports in the local newspapers. While I'm in Port Vila the *Vanuatu Daily Post* carries a banner headline on its front page, lamenting a national kava shortage. Spectacularly successful as an export, the crop has evidently been a victim of its own success as the supply of kava has been dramatically depleted, a local authority, Charlot Longwah reports in the paper. Known as 'green gold', Vanuatu kava is reputedly the most powerful in the South Pacific. Produced from the ground-up root of the pepper shrub (*Piper methysticum*), there is now little kava left to harvest. Hundreds of kava bars, called nakamal, are closing down, Mr Longwah laments, and many families who depend on the kava bar business 'to earn an extra income to sustain them or earn school fees for their children will be the group that will be most affected'. It takes from seven to fifteen years for a kava plant to be harvested, so in the meantime the aficionados may have to make do with that other brown water, Victoria Bitter.

The lead letter in the *Daily Post* is interesting too. It's written half in English and half in pidgin. It is (I think) on the subject of a local reggae band which is off to Europe, and reads:

*Dear Sir,*

*Mi stap read about tisfala new reggae group we hemi blo Vanuatu be hemi go bon lo Europe and hemi virtually unknown lo home country blong hem.*

*Mi no wan musician be stap wonder is this another doomed to failure short cut to look for fame and money scheme?*

*Mi stap listen lo old clips blo ol lo internet mo mi no laeken eni song blo olgeta.*

*Are they trying to force crap reggae music down the European's (sic) ears for the sake of quick fame and fortune, o hemi wan janis nom oblong turis olbaot lo Europe?*

*Sapos band is hemi no salem wan album yet lo Vanuatu, how nao bae hemi do well lo Europe we ol fans oli stap listen moa better bands and music.*

*It doesn't matter how much sugar and publicity the local and overseas media make of this band, it's the fans who will have the last say of their survival.*

*I wish them all the best in their endeavour in Europe and when they return home to face reality.*

*Lokal Fan*

Now Vanuatu's official national language, Bislama is a simple, strongly phonetic means of written and spoken communication. It's great fun to try to speak and decipher. For example, an enquiry after one's health is phrased, 'Yu oraet?'; a request to speak to the village chief runs, 'Mi wantem toktok long jif', the primary school is 'skul pikinini', and you can borrow a book from the 'Pablik Laebri'. If you understand Bislama you say, 'Mi savee', if you don't, you say 'Mi no savee'. It's like Esperanto, only much clearer.

I've been asked by an elderly friend – too embarrassed to ask his GP – if I can get him some Viagra in Port Vila, as in this part of the world you can usually buy it without a prescription. I go into the town's several pharmacies, but they don't appear to stock the product. Then, returning to the ship, I see a bearded Ni-Vanuatuan man in traditional costume wandering along, carrying a bow and arrow. He must have just finished a dance performance on the wharf for the passengers. As he looks like a man of the world, I stop and ask him where I can buy some Viagra. He throws back his head and roars with laughter at the question, then, still grinning, replies:

'Ni-Vanuatu fela no time need white fela Viagra. Ni-Vanuatu fela blong long-time hard-on, all-time big hard-on. Ni-Vanuatu fela no need Viagra.'

And just to make sure I've understood, he points with stabbing movements at his foot-long penis gourd. Mi savee.

# The Home-coming Traveller

Another journey completed, another notebook filled. Scraps, jottings, frustrations, impressions, observations. A memorable remark, a random encounter, a striking landscape, an overheard conversation, an altercation, a performance. The filled notebook joins the others in a drawer. Its contents will be put to use, eventually. The travel writer is like a home handyman who carefully saves every screw, nut, bolt and washer he finds, knowing that one day they will be put to some good use. But for the time being it's great to be home and back with the small domestic comforts the rest of the world can never provide: digging the garden, mowing the lawns, de-fleaing the cats, firing up the barbecue, drinks with family and friends.

But there will also come a time, not far distant, when I will reopen *The Times Atlas of the World*. Its maps will spellbind me yet again. Armenia, I wonder what that's like? Flick over a page. Turkey, I've always wanted to go there. Flick, flick. Sardinia, now there's a place I'd like to see. And Pesaro, where great-grandfather Luigi Berretti came from, I'd love to go there.

⌒

Another page, another journey, another notebook. Different ways to travel the world.